THE INTERNATIONAL POLITICS

OF INTELLIGENCE SHARING

THE INTERNATIONAL POLITICS
OF INTELLIGENCE SHARING

JAMES IGOE WALSH

COLUMBIA UNIVERSITY PRESS   NEW YORK

Columbia University Press
Publishers Since 1893
New York   Chichester, West Sussex

Copyright © 2010 Columbia University Press
All rights reserved

Library of Congress Cataloging-in-Publication Data
Walsh, James Igoe.
   The international politics of intelligence sharing / James Igoe Walsh.
      p.   cm.
   Includes bibliographical references and index.
   ISBN 978-0-231-15410-9 (cloth : alk. paper)
   ISBN 978-0-231-52088-1 (e-book)
   1. Intelligence service—International cooperation. I. Title.
   JF1525.I6.W38 2010
   327.12—dc22

                                                    2009019568

Columbia University Press books are printed on permanent and durable acid-free paper.
This book is printed on paper with recycled content.
Printed in the United States of America
c 10 9 8 7 6 5

CONTENTS

ACKNOWLEDGMENTS

Many people and institutions have made this book possible by sharing their intelligence and resources with me in the last few years. For their comments and suggestions on the ideas presented here, I thank Ted Arrington, Ersel Aydinli, Hans Born, Cynthia Combs, Björn Fägersten, Peter Gill, Michael Goodman, Loch Johnson, David Long, David Mendeloff, James A. Piazza, Richard R. Valcourt, Inger Weibust, Thorsten Wetzling, James Wirtz, Amy Zegart, and the anonymous reviewers for Columbia University Press. I am also grateful for feedback from individuals who participated in presentations of part of this work at Bilkent University, Carleton University, Syracuse University, and meetings of the American Political Science Association, the European Union Studies Association, the International Studies Association, and the European Consortium for Political Research.

The University of North Carolina at Charlotte gave me release time and funding to visit archives and libraries. My thanks to the librarians and archivists at the Harry S. Truman Library and Museum, the Lyndon Baines Johnson Presidential Library and Museum, the United States Army Center of Military History, the National Archives and Records Administration, and the National Security Archive for their assistance in locating sources and documents. Anne Routon of Columbia University Press made valuable suggestions about improving the manuscript and efficiently guided it to publication.

Parts of chapter 2 appeared in "Defection and Hierarchy in International Intelligence sharing. *Journal of Public Policy* 27, no. 2 (2007): 151–81 © Cambridge University Press and are reprinted here with permission. Portions of chapter 3 appeared in "Intelligence Sharing for Counterinsurgency," *Defense and Security Analysis* 24, no. 3 (2008): 281–301 © Taylor & Francis and are reprinted here with permission.

Special thanks are due to my parents, James and Elizabeth, for their support. I dedicate this book to my wife, Michelle, for her encouragement and intelligence in this and all things.

THE INTERNATIONAL POLITICS

OF INTELLIGENCE SHARING

CURVEBALL AND KSM

The charge that Iraq was actively developing chemical and biological weapons was an important rationale for the United States' invasion of the country in 2003. To make this charge, the United States needed some evidence about Iraqi weapons programs, but reliable evidence was difficult to obtain. Relations between the two countries had been very hostile since the Gulf War of 1991, so the United States did not have diplomats stationed in the country who could search for information about Iraqi weapons. The president of Iraq, Saddam Hussein, maintained a brutally tight grip over his society, and any scientist, government official, or military officer even suspected of sharing weapons information or otherwise collaborating with foreigners was very likely to be tortured and killed. The United States did control satellites and aircraft that could thoroughly reconnoiter Iraqi territory for weapons activity. But the Iraqis had learned to hide underground and out of sight those activities that they wanted to keep secret. During the 1990s, the United Nations closely monitored Iraq's military activities to ensure its compliance with provisions of the cease-fire ending the 1991 Gulf War that prohibited Iraq from developing weapons of mass destruction. These United Nations inspectors had been a valuable source of information about Iraqi activities, but Hussein expelled them in 1998.

This meant that the United States had very little capability itself to collect reliable information on Iraqi weapons development, so it turned to other countries to provide relevant intelligence. The German intelligence service, the Bundesnachrichtendienst (BND), shared information it had obtained from Rafid Ahmed Alwan. Alwan defected from Iraq to Germany in 1999 and was later interrogated by the BND, which, in an act of unintentional irony, gave him the code name Curveball. Curveball claimed that he had worked at a facility in Iraq that manufactured mobile biological weapons laboratories. Although the BND passed this information along to an American intelligence agency, it would not permit its American counterparts to question Alwan directly. Curveball's claims formed an important part of the American argument for war: Secretary of State Colin Powell drew on them for his presentation to the UN Security Council seeking international support for the invasion, and President George W. Bush mentioned mobile biological weapons labs in his State of the Union address just two months before the invasion.

Curveball had lied. He had lied about his educational credentials (claiming to have graduated first in his class at university when in fact he had graduated last), about the reasons why he left Iraq in 1999 (he was being investigated for embezzlement), and about his work history (he drove a taxi and worked for a television production company in Iraq). All his claims to have helped manufacture biological weapons labs—key building blocks in the American case for war—were fabrications. His lies were revealed after the invasion when no mobile labs or other evidence of a weapons of mass destruction program were discovered. Curveball had duped his German controllers and, more important, the Americans who based their decision for war partly on the intelligence he provided. How could such an error have occurred? Perhaps, as many commentators have argued, American leaders wanted war with Iraq and simply used Curveball's claims as a convenient justification.[1] A major part of the problem, however, was that Curveball was telling his falsehoods to the Germans, who in turn were sharing them with the Americans. This sharing made it difficult for the United States to verify to its own satisfaction that Curveball's story was reliable, even though many American intelligence personnel had doubts about his credibility. Because of the barriers that the United States faced in collecting intelligence on Iraq, it was very difficult to ignore a source of information provided by another country.

Curveball illustrates many of the promises and problems that states encounter when they seek to share intelligence. Receiving intelligence from another country may be the most efficient or, in some cases, the only source of information. This makes shared intelligence very valuable, as it provides at least some information that decision makers can use to reduce the uncertainty they inevitably face when crafting foreign policy. But it also means that the recipient is at the mercy of the state providing the intelligence. The sending state may manipulate the shared intelligence to serve its own purposes, or it may fail to properly confirm important pieces of the intelligence that it passes along. This vulnerability is compounded by the fact that shared intelligence is shrouded in great secrecy to keep its source hidden from outsiders, thus making it even more difficult for the receiving state to independently verify its accuracy. How do governments overcome these barriers and mutually benefit from sharing intelligence? That is the main question addressed in this book.

Another story illustrates the answer that this book provides. Khalid Sheikh Mohammed was a leader in the al Qaeda terrorist organization and the architect of the multiple attacks on the United States on September 11, 2001. Mohammed, often referred to in official American accounts as KSM, was captured in Pakistan in 2003. His capture was the result of years of careful investigation and the close cooperation of intelligence agencies in the United States, Pakistan, and other countries. Quite by accident, Philippine authorities discovered that KSM had been planning attacks from their country. Additional intelligence came from suspected terrorists captured after the September 11 attacks and interrogated by American authorities in Afghanistan and by other governments across the Middle East. Acting on information provided by a detainee, American intelligence agencies were then able to monitor telephone communications among members of KSM's organization in Pakistan. Someone with specific knowledge of his whereabouts gave this information to Pakistani officials. Although Pakistani forces were responsible for apprehending KSM, American officials were on the scene monitoring the situation. Pakistan then transferred KSM to American control, under which he was interrogated about his role in the September 11 attacks and other plots.[2]

This description of KSM's capture illustrates that intelligence sharing is not simply an additional source of useful information but can often be a requirement for successful action. Even though the United States had the technical means to track some of the communications of KSM or his associates, this was not sufficient to engineer his capture. In addition, the United States needed intelligence provided by detainees and agents controlled by other countries to piece together a sufficiently detailed map of KSM's activities. It needed the active cooperation of Pakistan in tracking KSM to his hideout in Rawalpindi. Intelligence sharing, therefore, can be a necessary part of successful foreign policy choices.

KSM's case also demonstrates how successful intelligence sharing can be tied to other forms of cooperation. To secure the cooperation of the Pakistani authorities, for example, the United States after September 11, 2001, gave the country enormous amounts of intelligence of its own as well as economic and military aid. Thus the United States helped secure Pakistan's willingness to supply the intelligence it needed by in turn providing Pakistan with its own intelligence as well as money and arms. Intelligence is a valuable commodity, and states bargain with one another to obtain the best possible return before agreeing to share it.

Finally, the United States worried that some countries might renege on their promises to share intelligence. Indeed, many of the countries that participated in the hunt for KSM may have had good reasons not to share their findings with the United States. For reasons discussed in chapter 5, Pakistan was especially suspect on this score. One step that the United States took to prevent such defection was closely supervising the pursuit of KSM. American officials collected some intelligence themselves, participated in organizing and carrying out the raid on the house where KSM was hiding, and insisted on taking custody of him. A key argument of my book is that such direct, hierarchical control of another state's counterterrorism and intelligence efforts is an important tool for overcoming the problem of defection from promises to share intelligence. Even though states may want to receive intelligence from others, the secrecy surrounding it makes it difficult for them to determine whether it has been shaded or manipulated in some way before it is shared. Accordingly, *hierarchy*—by which I mean some direct control over another state's intelligence activities—is a useful mechanism for overcoming such concerns about defection that has not been analyzed in existing works on sharing intelligence.

This book describes the benefits that states seek when they share intelligence, the barriers that they encounter when doing so, and the conditions under which forging a hierarchical relationship allows them to surmount these barriers. Intelligence sharing is a form of international cooperation, and we can learn much about the practice from explanations of cooperation developed for other domains. Intelligence sharing delivers to at least one participating state the benefits of more or better intelligence. The most important barrier to intelligence sharing is the fear that other participants will defect, in the sense of violating their agreement to cooperate, for example, by manipulating shared intelligence to serve their own ends. Moreover, the secrecy surrounding intelligence makes it very difficult for one state to tell when its partner has defected. This secrecy means that two common explanations of cooperation—mutual trust between participants, and the development of institutions and practices designed to provide information about compliance—are unlikely to be very effective in the area of intelligence sharing. Relational contracting, an alternative explanation of cooperation, has been applied to international politics and can add important insights to our understanding of the extent and nature of international intelligence sharing. Relational contracting is a part of transaction cost economics, which was first developed to explain the origins of business firms and was later applied to international politics and many other issues. Relational contracting draws attention to how states can incorporate hierarchical control, oversight, and monitoring mechanisms in their cooperative agreements in order to minimize defection by participants. Hierarchical agreements to share intelligence create a dominant state responsible for making important decisions and overseeing implementation. Such agreements also create the subordinate states that receive benefits such as shared intelligence, foreign aid, and protection from external threats in exchange for accepting the dominant state's control. Hierarchy allows states to overcome their concerns about defection and to engage in mutually beneficial cooperation. This is particularly useful in the area of intelligence sharing, as it otherwise is difficult for states to determine whether their partners are complying with an intelligence-sharing agreement.

INTELLIGENCE AND INTELLIGENCE SHARING

Intelligence is the collection, protection, and analysis of both publicly available and secret information, with the goal of reducing decision makers' uncertainty about a foreign policy problem.[3] Intelligence is a type of, but is not synonymous with, information. Intelligence is information, or a process of obtaining information, that someone prefers to be kept secret. The targets of intelligence collection and analysis keep information about their capabilities and intentions secret from others. Military forces are a common focus of other countries' intelligence efforts, and the targets of such intelligence collection try to mask their true capabilities and vulnerabilities in order to maintain the advantage of surprise over potential opponents. In turn, organizations charged with collecting intelligence on such targets do not reveal information about the sources and methods they use, since doing so would allow the targets to take countermeasures to secure their secrets from outsiders. Governments use secrecy to prevent others from knowing what they know or what actions they may take. But this understandable effort to secure secrets also makes it difficult for countries that agree to share intelligence to determine whether their partners are abiding by their commitments.

Intelligence is shared when one state—the sender—gives intelligence in its possession to another state—the recipient. Why do states share intelligence? Sharing intelligence is useful because decision makers often face a great deal of uncertainty when crafting foreign policy. They may be uncertain about the true intentions of friends and foes, the capabilities of others to deliver help or harm, the full range of policy options available to them, and the outcomes of implementing these policies. Intelligence about others' political intentions and material capabilities is especially important to the areas of defense and security policy, in which the results of policy errors—such as surprise attacks or entanglements in protracted military conflicts—can be very costly.[4] National governments devote substantial resources to collecting and analyzing intelligence. Nonetheless, decision makers are rarely satisfied with the quality and quantity of intelligence made available to them, and they often complain about the failure of intelligence agencies to anticipate important developments. This desire for intelligence is what leads governments to share intelligence with their counterparts overseas. The most important benefit from sharing intelligence is that it can give decision makers new perspectives on the problems they face and the likely effects of the policies they select.

What senders and recipients decide to exchange varies. Most countries share little or no intelligence with one another. In some cases, one state shares its intelligence in exchange for something else, such as foreign aid, security assurances, or diplomatic support. In other arrangements, the parties share intelligence with one another. Examples include pooling resources to analyze an intelligence target of interest to both countries, coordinating their networks of agents providing human intelligence, or jointly investing in new technologies to collect intelligence or in expensive intelligence assets such as satellites or listening posts. Agreements also vary in how extensively the parties share intelligence. In some relationships, such as that between the United States and Great Britain during the Second World War, the parties routinely share intelligence on a wide range of issues of mutual concern. Other agreements are more limited, with the parties sharing intelligence on some issues but not others. For instance, many current intelligence-sharing arrangements between the United States and countries in the Middle East and South Asia, which focus on intelligence concerning terrorist groups, take this form. Another way that intelligence-sharing agreements differ is how much one state directly controls another state's collection and analysis of intelligence. During the cold war, instead of direct control, the United States and Britain collaborated closely, but each retained the authority to determine its own intelligence activities. The United States, however, directly managed and oversaw West Germany's intelligence activities and, more recently, has supervised the restructuring of intelligence and security agencies in Latin America corrupted by drug-trafficking organizations.

The gains from sharing intelligence are greater if the participating states specialize. Specialization allows each to develop greater expertise regarding the targets and to create more focused and higher-quality collection and analysis techniques than one country could manage alone. Examples are countries that exchange intelligence from their signals intercept stations, reconnaissance aircraft, or satellites covering different areas of the world; that employ different means of collecting intelligence on the same target and sharing the results with one another; or that coordinate their networks of agents providing human intelligence so that they do not overlap. Cooperating states that agree to specialize in particular intelligence efforts can together generate more and better intelligence than would be possible if they each tried to provide adequate coverage of the same targets. This reasoning assumes that the intelligence resources developed for one target cannot be shifted at low cost to another target, which often is the case. For instance, a network of human intelligence agents providing information about one country or issue typically has little information about other countries or issues; listening posts for collecting signals intelligence are often aimed at particular targets and cannot be easily redirected to other targets; and analysts are trained in the language and history of one target and thus would require substantial retraining to address other targets.

SECRECY AND SHARING

Why might two states *not* share intelligence with each other? Often one country simply is not interested in another state's intelligence. Costa Rica, for instance, might have little to gain from sharing intelligence with Nepal. In other cases, though, two states could benefit from sharing. During the Second World War, the United States shared a great deal of intelligence with its allies Britain and Canada, but much less with another ally, the Soviet Union. But both the United States and the Soviet Union could have benefited by sharing more intelligence on German tactics, battle plans, or troop movements.[5] Why did they fail to realize these gains? Theories of international negotiation identify two general barriers to cooperation in such situations: the bargaining problem and the enforcement problem.[6] The bargaining problem pertains to disputes over how the participating states will share the costs and benefits of a cooperative arrangement, such as an agreement to share intelligence.[7] Governments may refuse to share intelligence if they cannot negotiate an agreement to apportion these costs and benefits acceptably. Then, once countries do agree on how to share intelligence, they must enforce the agreement. Some parties might have incentives to renege on their promises to share intelligence, and others must either prevent this or suffer the consequences.[8]

First consider the bargaining problem. Those states interested in sharing intelligence need to identify potential partners with useful intelligence, negotiate an agreement on what intelligence each will collect, how they will share it, whether they will offer any compensation such as military assistance or diplomatic assistance, and how much each state will invest in developing or redeploying intelligence resources to service the sharing agreement. Each of these issues provides benefits to one state and imposes costs on the other.

Countries may find it difficult to negotiate an agreement that divides these costs and benefits in a way that is acceptable to every participant. The first difficulty is the cost of negotiating. Each state must decide what intelligence it will send or wants to receive, the value of this intelligence, and the ability of its prospective partner to provide it. Each country will want the agreement to focus on its own priorities for intelligence collection and analysis. The participating countries also may have different preferences regarding quality control, human rights, and security standards. Countries with a strong tradition of protecting human rights, for example, might insist that their partners refrain from abusing these rights, and those without such protections might oppose such requirements as new and unnecessary burdens on their intelligence agencies. The participating states also have to construct a sharing arrangement that can withstand both anticipated and unforeseen contingencies, such as if the targets of the intelligence collection efforts unexpectedly change their behavior. Which state will pay which costs to set up and maintain the sharing agreement may also lead to disagreements. The intelligence-sharing agreement may try to benefit from specialization by calling for each country to concentrate on particular activities. Such specialization would require both countries to pay some costs to hire or retrain personnel and to invest in new equipment and technology, and they might differ over which country should pay for such changes.

The enforcement problem arises when states renege on a promise to share intelligence. Such a promise may be either deliberately broken with the approval of the relevant authorities or be involuntary in that lower-level state officials renege without such approval. For example, a sender may defect by altering or fabricating the intelligence it shares, withholding relevant intelligence, or exaggerating the accuracy of its sources. The motives for these forms of defection are the same: the sender manipulates the shared intelligence with the intention of influencing the recipient's subsequent actions. Or the defection may not be authorized by the government leadership. Individuals in a sending government may actually be operating under the control of another power or group that controls the intelligence they pass to other states. Corruption or other administrative weaknesses may limit a state's ability to collect intelligence efficiently in the first place. And the sending state may not share fully or honestly if some of its personnel disagree on political or policy grounds with the decision to share the intelligence. A recipient also can defeat the sender's interests by how it uses the shared intelligence. For instance, a recipient may deliberately share intelligence with a third party. This would constitute reneging, since intelligence-sharing agreements usually prohibit sharing with other states or actors. In such cases, the recipient believes that its interests are best served by passing along the intelligence in violation of the agreement, perhaps as a way to influence the third state's foreign policy, but the original sender most likely would not find this to be in its interests. A recipient also may inadvertently share intelligence with others. Individuals who have access to intelligence may be agents of a third state or other outside group and violate their government's policy by sharing intelligence with their controllers. Or officials in a receiving state may disagree with their government's policies, leading them either to publicize or fail to act on intelligence shared by another state. The sending state thus must worry about the loyalty of individuals and politically influential groups in the receiving state before it agrees to share intelligence.

The costs of defection can be great for both senders and receivers. Recipients may be deceived into providing valuable political, intelligence, and economic benefits to senders that reciprocate with poor intelligence. More important than this, however, are the indirect costs of cooperating with a sender that defects. A recipient may base important foreign policy decisions involving the use of force on flawed or misleading intelligence supplied by other states. The costs for the sending states can also be substantial. Recipients of their intelligence may either deliberately or inadvertently share vital secrets with hostile third parties or may reveal sources and methods of intelligence collection to enemies. These costs increase when the participating states have developed specialized and complementary intelligence efforts. Although such specialization increases the benefits produced by cooperation, it also raises the costs considerably if a partner defects. The most valuable partners—those with large quantities of valuable intelligence and with whom partners can develop complementary technical and human intelligence assets—can do the most damage when they renege on promises to share intelligence. The objective of specialization is to allow one partner to provide most of the coverage of a target of mutual interest, thereby freeing resources to be devoted to another target (or another purpose entirely). Defection can block access to the partner's specialized assets and seriously weaken its ability to gather useful intelligence on a target. Consider an arrangement in which two states agree to share intelligence on the same target country. One partner specializes in high-resolution reconnaissance images of the target's military facilities, and the other establishes a network of human agents in the target's government. Defection by either partner will harm the other's ability to generate a complete intelligence picture of the target. If the partner specializing in reconnaissance defects, perhaps by redirecting its imaging facilities to another target of more immediate interest, the other may be left with little reliable information about, say, the target's production of missiles. Conversely, if the state specializing in human intelligence defects, perhaps by failing to adequately secure its network from the target's counterintelligence operations, the other partner may lose valuable information about the goals or intentions of the target's leadership. Thus while specialization can offer many benefits, it also makes the partners far more vulnerable to defection.

The enforcement problem is a particularly powerful barrier to intelligence sharing because of the difficulties of determining whether a partner has defected. The three parts of the definition of intelligence provided earlier demonstrate how easy it is for states to defect without being detected. The first is the assumption that decision makers face uncertainty about important aspects of foreign policy, such as the true intentions or capabilities of another actor or the likely consequences of available policy options. Decision makers value and seek out intelligence provided by their own intelligence agencies or those of another state because it reduces this uncertainty. This uncertainty also creates a demand for intelligence that a sending state may be able to exploit by altering its intelligence to influence the receiving state's subsequent foreign policy choices.

Second, intelligence differs from raw information, or "facts," in that intelligence analyzes raw information, attempting to place it in the proper context and to use it to draw conclusions about those attributes of other actors or the state of the world that are not directly observable.[9] For example, intercepted signals traffic and other forms of electronic communication among military units may seem to need little interpretation. But even this intelligence source is largely meaningless without proper analysis:

Armed forces' and other messages are in specialized language which needs interpretation, and the intelligence interest is often less in what is being conveyed to the legitimate recipient than in what can be inferred. Uninteresting military administrative messages are the classic leads for reconstituting order-of-battle. Intercepted conversations on any subject are even more allusive and full of half-stated meanings. . . . For reasons of these kinds most of it needs a significant element of interpretation; good intelligence is never handed out on a plate.[10]

Decision makers in modern states rarely seek access to an individual piece of intelligence, instead relying heavily on their analysts to process such information. This analytical component of intelligence, however, can be more easily manipulated by the sending state than can the raw information on which it is based.

The third reason why an intelligence-sharing agreement is difficult to enforce has to do with the secret nature of intelligence. Intelligence draws on both open (publicly available) sources of information and secret or clandestinely obtained information. Governments have legitimate reasons to secure their intelligence activities so as to prevent their targets from discovering their sources and methods of collecting and analyzing intelligence. Consequently, intelligence agencies rarely reveal the full details of their sources, even to other agencies of the same government. This understandable concern with security poses a real problem for states trying to verify that their partners are complying with an agreement to share. That is, keeping secret many of the details of intelligence collection and analysis means that the sending state can easily alter or fabricate the information that it passes on to others, in order to influence their subsequent actions. Secrecy and security also create difficulties for sending states. The sending states want to ensure that recipients keep secure the intelligence that they share, for example, by limiting its distribution among government personnel and instituting effective safekeeping procedures. Likewise, the recipient governments want to keep these security efforts secret in order to prevent others from gaining access to their intelligence. But this secrecy also makes it difficult for the sending government to ensure that the security procedures are in fact protecting the secrets that it is sharing. This is the difference between the exchange of intelligence and the exchange of a tangible good. Tangible goods can be inspected after purchase to ensure that they conform to the buyer's expectations. But "buyers" of intelligence cannot easily monitor the "seller" to determine whether the intelligence it provides has been collected diligently and analyzed properly. Sellers of intelligence have difficulty ensuring that buyers are treating the intelligence as carefully as they should.

What We Know About Intelligence Sharing

How can states resolve the bargaining and enforcement problems of sharing intelligence? Many practitioners and scholars draw attention to mutual trust as the key to intelligence sharing.[11] Stéphane Lefebre writes that "trust in, and respect for, other [countries' intelligence] agencies is foremost when the time comes to decide on the extent of intelligence sharing arrangements" and that "confidence and trust are essential ingredients" for intelligence sharing. Chris Clough concludes that "mutual trust is the most important factor" driving sharing, and Derek Reveron holds that "engaging foreign intelligence services . . . requires high levels of trust on the part of all countries involved."[12] In regard to intelligence sharing, the most relevant definition of trust is the expectation by one state that the other state will not exploit its cooperation to secure immediate gains. How can states gain enough trust in each other that they will be willing to rely on the other's information? Different research traditions in political sociology, social psychology, social constructivism, and rational choice theory all cite similar interests as the principal condition for creating trust and thus sharing information.[13] The rationale is essentially the same for all these understandings of trust. A party will discount the value of shared information that it cannot verify itself when it suspects that its partner's interests diverge from its own. This divergence of interests may create an incentive to deliberately communicate incorrect intelligence to convince the receiver to select the action that will produce the outcome most favorable to the sender.

Although the argument that mutual trust facilitates intelligence sharing is powerful, it is important not to push it too far. These claims posit that trust is a necessary condition for intelligence sharing; that is, countries would not share intelligence if they did not trust each other. Lefebre's conclusion that trust is an "essential ingredient" for intelligence sharing and Clough's that it is the "most important factor" driving sharing suggest that trust must exist in order to share intelligence. But as this book later makes clear, countries may share intelligence even when they do not have much trust in each other. They do so by substituting a hierarchical relationship for trust. The United States managed, for example, to share intelligence with West Germany in the 1950s despite serious concerns about the Nazi pasts of the leaders of the German intelligence service, worries that the West German government might seek a rapprochement with the Soviet Union, and convincing evidence that the same government had been penetrated by Soviet spies. The United States also shared intelligence with its ally South Vietnam in the late 1960s and early 1970s, even though American officials could not trust their Vietnamese counterparts with any secret information about their war plans, knowing that it would soon be leaked to the enemy.

An alternative that addresses some of these concerns is liberal institutionalism. Liberal institutionalism seeks to understand the conditions under which states that do not have a great deal of trust in each other can nonetheless cooperate by deploying carefully crafted bargaining strategies aimed at reassuring its partner and by creating institutions to monitor for defection.[14] Liberal institutionalism has a more sophisticated and nuanced understanding of the conditions facilitating cooperation than do explanations that focus solely on trust. But its ability to explain intelligence sharing is limited by the fact that it assumes the international system is anarchic, in that it lacks a central authority to enforce agreements to cooperate. Liberal institutionalism instead holds that states can develop bargaining strategies and monitoring techniques to counter defection.

But secrecy makes it difficult to implement these measures for intelligence sharing. States interested in participating in a cooperative venture but worried about defection by other participants can ask an independent third party, such as an international organization, to monitor their compliance.[15] The international organization's evaluation of how well each state is complying with the cooperative agreement gives states the information they need in order to punish defectors.[16] But this option of an independent third party's monitoring compliance conflicts with states' desire to secure and keep secret their intelligence activities, since it requires that their intelligence agencies divulge detailed information about their actions. This explains why attempts at multilateral intelligence sharing through formal international organizations or ad hoc multilateral arrangements are so rare. States sharing intelligence in this way must calculate the likelihood of each of the other participants' defecting. They also must worry that the international organization itself might inadvertently or deliberately share intelligence with the other parties. It is much easier, therefore, for states desiring to share intelligence to do so with only one other participant to monitor.[17]

Another way that states can address concerns about enforcement is ensuring that a defection from cooperative agreement will harm the defecting state's reputation. Because a reputation for living up to promises is valuable, states with a reputation for defecting from agreements may find it more difficult to persuade other countries to cooperate with them. Sometimes the desire to maintain a reputation for honest dealing leads states to forgo the short-run benefits from defection.[18] But maintaining a good reputation influences this choice only if the state knows that its decision will be communicated to other states. These concerns about security complicate efforts to reassure partners, however, because the details of most intelligence-sharing arrangements are kept secret from third parties. This makes it difficult for one partner to hurt another's reputation by accusing it of defection, since doing so necessitates revealing details about the intelligence that has, or was supposed to have, been shared.

Hierarchy and Intelligence Sharing

How can states overcome the barriers to share intelligence, especially when they do not completely trust one another? Transaction costs economics provides an answer that does not rely on mutual trust, international institutions, or reputations. Transaction cost economics was initially developed to explain why individuals create and join a particular type of hierarchical organization—the business firm—to govern their interactions rather than relying on exchange through the marketplace.[19] The relevant insight was that firms do not exist simply to produce goods and services but also to manage the relations among their members by creating hierarchical relationships in which owners and managers exercise considerable direct control over their subordinates. Scholars have begun to refine and apply the insights of transaction cost economics to many other domains, including international politics. This application draws most intensively on the branch of transaction cost economics known as relational contracting, which analyzes situations like international politics in which the parties cannot rely on a third party, such as a court or an effective international organization, to prevent them from

reneging on their promises. Instead, relational contracts lead to cooperation only when they are self-enforcing, that is, when they are designed so
that no party has an incentive to renege. Scholars have drawn on insights
from transaction cost economics to explain, for example, the different
organizations of the North Atlantic Treaty Organization and Warsaw
Pact alliances during the cold war, the varying forms of United States'
military cooperation during the twentieth century, and the organization
of colonial empires.[20]

Transaction cost economics addresses the puzzle of why actors that
could gain from cooperating with one another sometimes fail to do so.
The key variables are the number, type, and extent of transaction costs
that the parties must pay to sustain their cooperation. The existence and
size of these transaction costs influence both the likelihood that the actors
will cooperate and the agreements and institutions they create to govern
their relationships. If the transaction costs are much lower than the mutual gains produced by cooperation, exchange is most efficiently arranged
through arm's-length transactions like market exchanges. Actors have no
incentive to cooperate if the transaction costs exceed the benefits that
would be produced by their exchange. Finally, when the transaction costs
are substantial but still smaller than the possible gains from cooperation,
actors devise hierarchical institutions to govern their relations.

Parties hoping to cooperate must pay the costs associated with bargaining, which, as we have seen, involves negotiating an agreement with
others. They also must pay enforcement costs, which include the costs of
ascertaining whether the partners are living up to their promises to share
intelligence and punishing those that are not. These costs increase when
the actors make regular and frequent exchanges, as each instance of cooperation requires the payment of some transaction costs. They also increase
when the actors must specialize in order to undertake the transaction, as
this requires each actor to shift its assets away from their current use to
new uses specific to the needs of the cooperative venture. Transaction
costs are greater, too, when the actors face more uncertainty about how
their environment might change in the future, as this means they must
negotiate more complex agreements and monitor more developments.

Bargaining and enforcement, the two barriers to intelligence sharing, are transaction costs that, if large enough, may prevent states from
engaging in otherwise mutually beneficial sharing. And these costs are
likely to be large for intelligence sharing, for the three reasons—sustained

cooperation, specialization, and uncertainty—identified by transaction cost economics. States sharing intelligence often want to sustain this co-operation, since a continuous flow of high-quality intelligence that can be regularly incorporated into decision making is easier to manage than is negotiating individual arrangements for each bit of shared informa-tion. Intelligence sharing also is often characterized by specialization, in which each participating country develops an expertise in one aspect of the joint intelligence collection and analysis. And uncertainty, too, plays a very large role in intelligence generally and in intelligence sharing par-ticularly. Uncertainty is the main reason for seeking intelligence in the first place. Most important is the uncertainty about a partner's interest in defecting from a promise to share intelligence, since this defection is very difficult to detect.

Relational contracting differs from liberal institutionalism in that it does not assume that the international system is completely anarchic in the sense that it lacks any authority that can punish defection from promises to coperate.[21] Even though sovereign states may be formal and legal equals, in practice they can and do develop hierarchical institu-tions that, in contradiction to the anarchy assumption, enable one state to manage and oversee some of the other participants' activities.[22] The dominant party in a hierarchical relationship is responsible for making the major decisions, and the subordinate party or parties recognize the authority of the dominant party and are responsible for complying with these decisions.[23] A hierarchy gives the dominant state three kinds of authority over the actions of the subordinate state.[24] First, a hierarchy gives the dominant state the right to interpret the agreement to share intelligence, which minimizes the subordinate state's opportunities to exploit ambiguities and unexpected developments. Second, a hierarchy allows the dominant state to create and maintain oversight mechanisms to ensure the subordinate state's compliance with the terms of their intelligence-sharing agreement. Third, the acceptance of a hierarchical relationship by a subordinate partner means that it has given the domi-nant state the right to punish defection without the subordinate state's having the right to retaliate.

Under the right conditions, a hierarchy allows participants to address the bargaining and enforcement problems of initiating and maintaining an intelligence-sharing relationship. The bargaining problem concerns how the gains from and the costs of sharing intelligence are parceled out among the participating states. One aspect of the bargaining problem is deciding how to collect and secure intelligence. Countries that are contemplating sharing intelligence with each other may have different collection priorities and security standards. Consider American intelligence sharing with South Vietnam, a case discussed in more detail in chapter 3. Both countries wanted information about their common enemy: the government of North Vietnam and the rebels it supported that operated against the South Vietnamese government. But the United States and South Vietnam attached different priorities to different types of intelligence, as well as to the procedures or standards to be followed in collecting and analyzing this intelligence. The United States worried that corruption and internal political differences could lead South Vietnamese officials to pass along the shared intelligence to the enemy and therefore preferred that their sharing arrangement require the South Vietnamese to improve their internal security and counterintelligence efforts. The United States also was more reluctant to officially sanction the use of torture against suspected rebels as a tool to gain intelligence, whereas the South Vietnamese routinely practiced torture.

Bargaining differences like these are more easily resolved when one participant's influence and contribution are more important to the success of the joint venture than the other's. This allows the standards and procedures of the more powerful state to take precedence over those of the other participants. The dominant state sets the standards for both political and efficiency reasons. The state that brings the most material resources to the intelligence-sharing arrangement typically has more options for collecting intelligence outside the arrangement, either on its own or in collaboration with third states. This means that it is less sensitive to the benefits of sharing intelligence with any one partner and is able to resist a partner's demands by credibly threatening to abandon the relationship. It also means that together the participants have to make fewer changes to standardize their collection, analysis, and security procedures. Because it sets the standards of the arrangement, the dominant state does not have to pay the costs of adhering to the others' standards. Although the subordinate states do have to pay these costs, their total costs should be smaller because they contribute less to the overall venture than the dominant state does.[25]

A hierarchical relationship also addresses other bargaining costs that the participants must pay to establish and maintain the intelligence-sharing relationship. The most valuable arrangements are those in which the participating states specialize in their collection and analysis. Specializing requires redeploying existing human and physical resources, for example, by purchasing new intelligence collection technology and retraining or hiring new intelligence personnel. These start-up costs often are substantial, especially for smaller countries. The dominant state, which controls more resources, can smooth the smaller states' path to participation by agreeing to pick up many of these costs. Another source of substantial costs are changes in the target's actions. That is, the target may change its behavior or introduce new security procedures that make ineffective the existing methods of collecting intelligence against it, thus requiring the states to invest in new and different means of collecting intelligence. The dominant state's control of more resources allows it to subsidize its subordinates' efforts to adapt to unexpected changes.

Although partners to an intelligence-sharing arrangement carefully assess the likelihood that the other participants will defect, it often is difficult to distinguish between those that will observe the terms of a sharing arrangement and those that will not. Creating a hierarchical relationship helps reduce this uncertainty by giving both the dominant and the subordinate states defenses against defection. The states can structure their agreements to minimize the chances and costs of defection by other participants. They can limit the intelligence they share to specific targets or sources on which the participating states' interests are most closely aligned and not share intelligence on issues in which their interests conflict. Limiting intelligence sharing to issues of common concern reduces the participating states' incentive to renege. A second and closely related way to limit defection is to specify the targets and types of intelligence that participants will share. This helps create an unambiguous and mutually agreed-on standard that can be used to determine what actions do and do not constitute reneging. By acknowledging that the participating states' interests may diverge sufficiently to create irresistible benefits from defection, the agreement can be structured to avoid such situations.

Three additional steps reduce the chance of defection by introducing an element of hierarchy into the relationship and limiting the subordinate state's decision-making autonomy. Without some sort of monitoring, the sending state can fabricate or manipulate shared intelligence at little cost and without the knowledge of the receiving state. Conversely, it is easy for recipients to send shared intelligence to third parties without the knowledge of the sharing state. The hierarchical solution to this problem is to have the dominant state's intelligence services directly monitor the actions of their partners in the subordinate states. For example, the dominant country's intelligence services might require their counterparts to hand over some of the raw information on which they base their conclusions so that its accuracy can be evaluated, or they could compare shared intelligence with other intelligence before using it for any foreign policy decisions. In other cases, the dominant state may insist on directly managing the other country's intelligence service, supervising the activities of their counterpart's collection activities, and vetting the sources and employees of their partner's services. The dominant state may assign its personnel to policymaking or operational tasks in the subordinate state's agencies. Such personnel are usually described as technical advisers, and they certainly are in a position to give the subordinate state relevant knowledge. But their primary loyalty is not to the subordinate state, or even to norms of their field of expertise, but to the dominant state that assigned them to this role. The dominant state's direct involvement in the policymaking and operations of the subordinate state gives it detailed knowledge of how well the subordinate state is collecting and analyzing intelligence.

Dominant states may also include hierarchical elements in the agreement that raise the costs of defection. Participants accused of cheating can, of course, be threatened with the termination of benefits, such as shared intelligence. Hierarchical intelligence-sharing arrangements can give the dominant state additional leverage. For example, they often provide subordinates with "back channels" to top government officials for bilateral negotiations on other issues that can be halted when the subordinate defects. The dominant state also often directly or indirectly finances its partner's collection and analysis of intelligence. Providing financing gives the subordinate state more resources to carry out policies, and the dominant state targets the money to those policies that will serve its interests. But strings are always attached to such money. The subordinate state must use the money only for the purposes specified by the dominant state; it may be required to provide matching funds; and it must promise to supply accounting and other evidence that the funds have been expended in the manner intended. This oversight also gives the dominant state a window on other, related actions by the subordinate state. For example, the dominant state may be concerned that the subordinate will use its funds to replace rather than supplement its funding of some activities. Accordingly, the agreement to provide financing should require the subordinate state to furnish budgetary data addressing this concern. These data also are useful to the dominant state to construct a more comprehensive picture of the subordinate state's actions and priorities. Financing also is a useful tool for punishing defection, allowing the dominant state to withdraw the money or shift it to other purposes if it discovers that the subordinate has cheated on the agreement.

Finally, national governments can restructure the intelligence and security bureaucracies in countries with which they share intelligence. Dominant states can use their superior wealth and knowledge to create incentives for the subordinate government to, for example, reform its security agencies in ways that ensure that staff support the state's foreign policy. One such way is training. The objective of training and restructuring is to give subordinate states the technical knowledge and skills needed to implement policy more effectively. Training and restructuring also can serve as an indirect form of monitoring. Training socializes students from other states into the training state's goals and routines. The dominant state can also give its partners funds, equipment and technology, and organizational blueprints to alter their agencies. The motive is to replace existing agencies that do not share the dominant state's objectives with new agencies that do. Military training is a good example. Powerful states often offer training and education opportunities to military personnel from other states. The goals are teaching technical skills and, often, the norms of the training state. Military training by the United States and other Western countries during the cold war often emphasized anticommunism as an important policy goal. Since the end of the cold war, such training instead encourages respect for human rights and civilian control.

Subordinate states must also worry about defection by their dominant partner. Because the dominant partner is more powerful, its defection can inflict substantial harm on the subordinate. Accordingly, subordinate states prefer their intelligence-sharing arrangement to include provisions that reduce the costs and risks of defection by the dominant partner. One way to address this concern is to add a "risk premium" to the dominant power's political and economic compensation to its subordinate partner. Here the dominant partner gives the subordinate resources that exceed the value of sharing intelligence in order to compensate for the large cost if the dominant state later defects. The dominant power may also include provisions that would make it more costly to exploit the junior partner. One way of reassuring the subordinate state is to encourage it to specialize in some aspects of collecting and analyzing the intelligence. As we have seen, such specialization is often one of the major benefits available from intelligence sharing, as it allows each participant to focus on the intelligence collection and analysis of targets and functions to which it can add the most value. For the same reason, specialization gives subordinate partners greater influence over the dominant state. The dominant state's specialized intelligence activities have far less value alone than when combined with the subordinate's specialized efforts. When faced with the defection of a dominant state, the subordinate can threaten to stop cooperating and thus end the stream of benefits that the dominant state receives from their joint intelligence operations.

The dominant state must command considerable political and economic resources of value to the subordinate state, as well as resources to punish a subordinate state that defects. Because subordinate states must surrender some freedom of maneuver and submit to the decisions of and monitoring by the dominant power, it is important to understand how relational contracting understands this disparity of power. First, some suggest that powerful states *always* insist on creating hierarchical arrangements that give them the right to manage and interpret the relationship between the two countries.[26] Relational contracting holds, in contrast, that only in some circumstances do powerful states want to use their resources to create a hierarchical arrangement and that in other circumstances, they prefer either to forgo cooperation with a particular partner or to cooperate using more anarchic arrangements. The reason is that creating and managing a hierarchical relationship is costly for the dominant state. Therefore, when partnering with a state unlikely to defect, dominant states prefer less or even no hierarchy in their relationship. The desire for an expensive hierarchical relationship thus increases with the subordinate state's likelihood of defection.

Second, subordinate states prefer to avoid the restrictions on their actions that hierarchy imposes.[27] But this often is unrealistic, for often the dominant state will agree to cooperate only if the subordinate accepts the limits of a hierarchy. Powerful states are powerful because they have other ways to satisfy the same objectives as cooperation would. For example, if a subordinate states refuses a request from the powerful United States that it share intelligence, the United States can use its resources to develop other sources of intelligence, such as satellites or sharing with other countries in the region. Subordinate states recognize and accept their inferior status because doing so offers mutually beneficial cooperation with the dominant state by minimizing the chances that either party will defect. In exchange for accepting their subordinate status, such states may receive economic aid, intelligence, or protection from external threats from the dominant state. Submission to a hierarchical relationship allows the subordinate state to reassure the dominant state of its willingness to comply with the intelligence-sharing agreement and ensures that it will continue to accrue such benefits. In such situations, participation in a hierarchy may be the best available outcome for subordinate states, which must choose between cooperating on the terms preferred by the dominant state or not cooperating at all and seeing the dominant state pursue other means of achieving its objectives.[28]

Not all intelligence-sharing relationships are characterized by hierarchy. What leads to a hierarchical relationship? Relational contracting expects that the actors will agree to form a hierarchical relationship when the benefits that each will receive from this arrangement exceed the expected bargaining costs of negotiating the agreement, the expected costs of defection by a partner in the hierarchy, and the costs the actor must pay to maintain the hierarchy. Hierarchical arrangements are most useful and thus most likely when cooperation offers benefits and a hierarchy can be created relatively cheaply.

Creating a hierarchical intelligence-sharing arrangement has three steps. First, a recipient must be convinced that a potential sender has access to valuable and accurate intelligence, since this is the primary benefit from such cooperation. The value of the shared intelligence to the recipient must be greater than the costs of any reciprocal benefits, such as diplomatic support, foreign or military aid, or intelligence. Little or no sharing occurs if the recipient or sender sees only modest benefits in cooperation. Second, if the perceived costs and likelihood of defection are much smaller than the benefits of cooperation, the states will prefer an "anarchic" intelligence-sharing arrangement. This arrangement spells out the intelligence that the sender is expected to provide and the reciprocal benefits that the recipient will offer in exchange, but it lacks the costly hierarchical monitoring or enforcement measures that impinge on either partner's decision-making autonomy. If one state fears that the other may defect, as the third step it will create a hierarchical agreement to govern the intelligence-sharing arrangement. A hierarchy is attractive if the costs of creating and maintaining it are less than the benefits of having access to shared intelligence. If not, the participant worried about defection by its partner will simply decline to share intelligence.

This discussion clarifies the differences between the relational contracting explanation of intelligence sharing put forward here and the trust and liberal institutionalism explanations of cooperation, which focus on the first two steps. According to the trust approach to cooperation, only two conditions are necessary to share intelligence: the participants believe they will benefit from sharing intelligence, and they trust each other not to defect. But states have great difficulty determining whether their partners have reneged on promises to share intelligence. This in turn leads them to limit their sharing to only those states with interests very similar to their own, as then the partner has fewer incentives to defect. Liberal institutionalism holds that the participating countries may still decide to cooperate if they can raise the costs of defection, by targeting the defecting state's reputation or having a third party monitor its compliance. Liberal institutionalism downplays the opportunities for and consequences of creating hierarchical institutions in international politics. Instead, it maintains that a state will simply avoid striking bargains with potential partners viewed as likely to defect if it has no suitable reputational and monitoring mechanisms, as is often the case for intelligence sharing.

Relational contracting holds that states have more options when seeking to cooperate. That is, participants can create hierarchical institutions to govern their relations and minimize a partner's ability to defect if the costs of hierarchy for both the dominant and subordinate states are less than the benefits they will receive by sharing intelligence. We thus are likely to see more cooperation in international sharing than the trust and liberal institutionalism approaches expect, because even those states that are quite wary of each other's motives may be able to develop hierarchical arrangements to govern their relations in a mutually beneficial way.

The insights derived from relational contracting lead to four expectations. First, potentially large gains are a necessary condition for intelligence sharing. Because it is difficult for states to determine whether their partners are defecting from or complying with an intelligence-sharing arrangement, they should share intelligence only when they conclude that the gains from doing so are clearly larger than the potential costs of defection.

Second, assuming that such gains are available and that both states estimate the other's incentives to defect are low, they will share intelligence through anarchic institutions. This expectation is consistent with both the trust perspective on intelligence sharing and liberal institutionalism. States that trust each other have little need to construct elaborate defenses against defection. The institutions they create to facilitate intelligence sharing place few constraints on each participant's decision-making independence and instead focus on developing efficient technical practices and standards for the exchange of information.

Third, if at least one state estimates that the other's incentives to defect are high, it will construct a hierarchical relationship to govern intelligence sharing if the benefits from sharing are greater than the costs of creating and maintaining the hierarchy plus the (now reduced) costs of defection. Hierarchy reduces the likelihood of defection by giving the dominant state the authority to monitor its subordinate and by making it more difficult for the dominant state to exploit its subordinate. Because these measures are expensive to create and maintain, states should consider them only when the benefits of intelligence sharing are worthwhile.

Fourth, power imbalances are a necessary but not a sufficient condition for creating a hierarchy. The dominant state needs to control more resources than the subordinates do so that it can reward them for giving up some of their decision-making autonomy and also to be able to threaten to punish those that do defect. Powerful states do not always insist on hierarchical relationships but seek hierarchy only when they conclude that the costs of creating and managing the hierarchical relationship are smaller than the gains from sharing intelligence.

Evaluating the Argument

This argument makes novel contributions to how we understand intelligence sharing. It posits that states can develop hierarchical relationships to govern their intelligence-sharing relationships, a possibility that has not been investigated elsewhere. It spells out the conditions under which states are likely to create and sustain such hierarchies. According to this argument, these conditions are not rare, and thus intelligence sharing should be more common and successful than other explanations would expect.

How much actual intelligence sharing does this approach explain? Most of this book addresses this question by using case studies. My empirical investigation differs from those most commonly used in the area of intelligence studies.[29] Many studies of intelligence matters are written by historians, who are most interested in developing a full narrative of particular cases.[30] Their work has the great advantage of relying on primary sources of evidence, especially declassified documents, and I follow this practice as well. Historians' focus on narrative and primary sources leads them to analyze episodes of successful intelligence sharing for which many sources can be obtained,[31] which often is difficult because governments are typically reluctant to discuss their intelligence-sharing practices. Policy concerns are another important motive for work on this topic, leading to many analyses that explore recent intelligence developments and provide guidance for avoiding recent problems. As with historical investigation, this can lead to analyzing only few types of intelligence sharing.

In this book I use a social scientific approach, meaning that my empirical investigation directly and deliberately evaluates the explanatory power of my theoretical argument. My case studies directly compare the empirical findings and expectations of mutual trust, neoliberal institutionalism, and relational contracting with the goal of identifying the strengths and weaknesses of each in explaining outcomes of interest. I also select cases that shed the most analytical light on each of these explanations, using the "most similar" method of case selection and comparison. Most similar cases are similar in regard to most influences on intelligence sharing. They differ mainly in one of the influences on sharing identified by relational contracting: the mutual gains available from cooperation, the likelihood of defection, and the net costs of hierarchy. These differences allow me to make controlled comparisons that permit conclusions about how the presence or absence of a particular characteristic influences the likelihood that states will or will not share intelligence.[32] Because I use a great deal of primary evidence, such as declassified government documents and correspondence among decision makers, I can also check the validity of the relational contracting expectations advanced here through process tracing. Process tracing involves delving into the details of a case to determine whether decision makers actually took into account the causal factors identified by relational contracting when deciding if and how they should share intelligence. If my explanation is correct, the detailed history of decision making in each case should reflect these causes, and not causes identified by other explanations of cooperation.[33]

The last chapter compares all the cases analyzed in the book. Overall I found that the relational contracting explanation of intelligence sharing is promising but not perfect. Hierarchy, it turns out, is frequently used to structure intelligence sharing. Some, but not all, of my conclusions from most-similar comparisons and from process tracing support my expectations about the conditions under which hierarchy is used. This reasonable but not perfect level of support for the expectations is, I believe, a positive development. It would be unrealistic to expect that any explanation of a complex social phenomenon like intelligence sharing would be strongly supported in each case. My attention to the careful research design that produced these findings means that there is considerable room for future research to refine, or perhaps challenge, my arguments.

The final chapter also discusses three implications of my findings for the study of intelligence and for intelligence reform and policy. Many who study intelligence, or national security policy more broadly, are suspicious of theory. They argue that theory distracts from pressing moral and policy concerns and has little power to illuminate concepts and problems that can be easily apprehended by direct observation. Nonetheless, the application of social scientific approaches to the study of intelligence can yield valuable insights.[34] For example, the relational contracting explanation of intelligence sharing draws on a larger body of theory about the sources and types of cooperation. It identifies hierarchy as an important solution to barriers to cooperation. Hierarchy has not been previously discussed in any detail in regard to intelligence sharing. A carefully developed theory can make an important contribution to our understanding of the possibilities for and limitations of intelligence sharing.

This theory also has implications for how we evaluate current policy and proposals for policy reform. The concluding chapter briefly considers two such implications. The first is the fact that the United States frequently shares intelligence with other states that systematically abuse human rights. It often is argued that such cooperation with human rights–abusing states is counterproductive. For example, in the current American effort against Islamic terrorism, close intelligence cooperation with states that do not respect human rights, such as Egypt and Saudi Arabia, may actually drive more people to support such terrorist movements. Relational contracting can help explain why the United States creates and maintains such seemingly counterproductive relationships. Even though these countries possess intelligence of value to the United States, it cannot trust them to share intelligence fully or reliably and so has formed hierarchical intelligence-sharing relationships. This gives the United States greater control over the subordinate's state's intelligence activities, but at the cost of effectively supporting unpopular and inhumane local governments. There is thus a strong and direct trade-off between sharing intelligence effectively, supporting human rights, and sustaining popular support for the United States. A second implication of relational contracting concerns the reform of the U.S. intelligence agencies themselves. Many people believe that these agencies rely far too heavily on technical means of collecting intelligence, such as reconnaissance satellites and the interception of communications, and should strengthen their ability to collect "human intelligence" from agents, defectors, and refugees. One way to collect more human intelligence is to establish sharing relationships with other countries that can collect this intelligence for the United States. But this exposes the United States to possible defection by these partners. A better alternative, many argue, is to expand the ability of U.S. intelligence agencies to collect this human intelligence themselves. These prescriptions, however, overlook an alternative option: expanding *hierarchical* relations with other states. Hierarchy can allow the United States to more closely supervise the intelligence collection practices of subordinate states, making it more difficult for them to defect. Expanding such hierarchical relationships might be a more cost-effective way to quickly increase the quantity and quality of human intelligence available to American authorities.

During the first decades of the cold war, the United States shared much intelligence with Britain, decided against sharing much intelligence with France, and relied on West Germany for some intelligence while carefully monitoring and controlling its activities. These decisions correspond closely to each country's incentives to defect and the net benefits to the United States of creating a hierarchical structure to govern intelligence sharing.

From the American perspective, Britain had valuable intelligence assets and was very trustworthy; therefore much was to be gained from sharing intelligence, with little need for a hierarchical relationship. France, however, had little accurate intelligence and could not be completely trusted. Even though the United States could have created a hierarchical relationship to monitor France's activities, the little valuable intelligence it could provide meant that the costs of maintaining such a hierarchy would be greater than the benefits the United States would receive. What became West Germany's intelligence service had the potential to provide useful intelligence but was of questionable reliability. Here the United States did negotiate a hierarchical sharing agreement because the benefits of shared German intelligence outweighed the costs of the hierarchy.

The German case most clearly illustrates how relational contracting sheds new light on the practice of intelligence sharing. The other

explanations discussed in chapter 1, trust and neoliberal institutionalism, do not envision hierarchical relationships in international politics
and thus would expect the United States not to share intelligence with
West Germany. In contrast, relational contracting expects that under
such conditions, the United States would be able to benefit from German
intelligence and resolve some of the problems of possible German defection by creating a hierarchy.

Analyzing cold war intelligence offers valuable methodological rewards. The cold war is now history, and national governments, especially
that of the United States, have declassified much information on foreign
policy and intelligence matters. Access to these internal documents thus
offers many details about intelligence sharing and political relations during this period, allowing an assessment of why decision makers chose
to cooperate with some states but not others. I relied heavily on contemporary internal documents—most created by the State Department
and the Central Intelligence Agency (CIA)—interpreting the internal
security and political situations in Britain, France, and West Germany
and their intelligence capabilities and foreign policy priorities. Especially
important are the many American government documents concerning
cooperation with the newly formed West German intelligence organization that have recently been declassified as part of an investigation into
links between American intelligence and war criminals in the early cold
war period.[1] These cases are also consistent with the guidelines for other,
most-similar comparisons discussed in chapter 1. Other potential influences on cooperation that are not of great interest here, such as the larger
political conflict of the cold war rivalry between the United States and
the Soviet Union and the fact that all three countries were democracies,
are held roughly constant across the cases. The principal variation is in
factors identified by the relational contracting, trust, and liberal institutional explanations of cooperation.

This chapter first describes the United States' key interests and concerns in European security and politics in the early cold war era. It then
analyzes the intelligence capabilities, internal security and foreign policy
interests, and outcomes for Britain, France, and West Germany for sharing with the United States. The conclusion draws on the case materials
to describe what drove the Americans' decisions to share intelligence and
how they structured their sharing arrangements.

American Intelligence in the Early Cold War

At the close of the Second World War in 1945, the administrations of President Franklin D. Roosevelt and then Harry Truman did not have strongly held ideas about their interests in postwar European security beyond a desire to continue some sort of cooperation with their major wartime allies, Britain and the Soviet Union. But by early 1947 the Truman administration had defined the United States' paramount interest as ensuring that continental Europe would not be dominated by a hostile great power. Germany and the Soviet Union were seen as having the economic and military potential to become European hegemons. Because defeated Germany was occupied by the United States and its allies, France and Britain, as well as the Soviet Union, it posed little immediate threat. Instead, the Truman administration saw the Soviet Union as the most significant challenge. Although analysts of the cold war largely agree that the United States wanted to prevent a hostile power from controlling Europe's economic and military resources, they differ on the reasons the United States attached such importance to this goal. Some hold that the most important source of conflict between the United States and the Soviet Union was whether one or the other superpower would control postwar Germany.[2] Others believe that the United States was interested in ensuring that it would have privileged access to Western Europe's markets.[3] Yet another group of scholars views the superpowers' different political ideologies—communism for the Soviet Union and democratic capitalism for the United States—as the force driving their cold war competition.[4]

The United States pursued three major policies to secure its interests in Europe. The first was the creation of a pro-American government in West Germany. During the war, the United States, the Soviet Union, France, and Britain agreed that each would temporarily occupy a section of defeated Germany, and then negotiate a mutually acceptable status for the country after the cessation of hostilities. By late 1947, however, the Truman administration concluded that it would be impossible to agree with the Soviet Union on this issue and proceeded to create the Federal Republic of Germany out of the western zones occupied by the United States, Britain, and France. The Soviet Union followed by transforming its eastern occupation zone into the German Democratic Republic.

The second major policy was the creation of the North Atlantic Treaty Organization (NATO), negotiated in early 1948 between the United States and the countries of Western Europe. The creation of NATO signaled a fundamental change in American foreign policy, permanently committing the United States to the security of continental Europe. American participation in NATO also reassured Western Europe that the United States would prevent the new West German government from pursuing a foreign policy or forming armed forces that could threaten its neighbors, as well as providing an American counterweight to the presence of the large Soviet military forces stationed in Eastern Europe.

The third policy was the economic reconstruction of Western Europe. The United States' Marshall Plan of 1947 helped finance the rebuilding of Western Europe and encouraged the recipients to lower barriers to intra-European trade and investment. (The Marshall Plan, named for U.S. Secretary of State George C. Marshall, was a cooperative effort by the United States and many nations of Western Europe to boost their economic recovery.) The plan's principal security objective was shoring up support for pro-American political parties and reducing the attractiveness of indigenous Communist parties seen as following the lead of the Soviet Union.

The United States' interests and policies regarding postwar European security shaped the types of intelligence the American government sought. The United States needed accurate intelligence on the Soviet bloc's political intentions, military plans and capabilities, and research and development of new military technologies such as atomic weapons and long-range missiles. The fact that the Soviet Union and its allies in Eastern Europe were largely closed to foreigners meant that the primary sources of accurate intelligence for the United States were the interception of radio and other signals from the Soviet bloc and information from refugees and defectors from Eastern Europe. Western European countries had much better access to these intelligence resources than did the United States, as most defectors and especially refugees from the Soviet bloc fled westward. Listening posts in Western Europe could intercept communications in much of Eastern Europe and the western Soviet Union, whereas the United States could not effectively monitor these regions from its own territory. Nonetheless, the United States worried about sharing intelligence with governments in Europe with foreign policy interests quite different from its own and with those with signifi-cant domestic Communist influence.

BRITAIN

Benefits of Sharing Intelligence

Britain had three assets that made its intelligence collection and analysis efforts useful to the United States. First, British intelligence services in effect ran their Canadian and Australian counterparts. In the early post-war period, the Australian signals intelligence organization was led and staffed by members of Britain's main signals intelligence organization, the Government Communication Headquarters (GCHQ), and the senior official of the Canadian organization was supported by GCHQ. Britain thus brought to its cooperation with the United States its own intel-ligence capabilities as well as the (much smaller) capabilities of Canada and Australia.[5]

Second, Britain's experience as a colonial power gave it access to territories around the world that were useful for collecting intelligence on the Soviet Union. During the early cold war period, technical intelligence-gathering capabilities, such as signals intelligence listening posts and facilities for clandestine aerial surveillance of Soviet-controlled territory, were a very important means of collecting politically and mili-tarily useful intelligence. Because the Soviet Union and its clients were largely closed to foreigners, it was difficult for the United States to use diplomats, attachés, and travelers not affiliated with the American gov-ernment to gather significant intelligence. Moreover, the Eastern Euro-pean states' powerful and suspicious internal security apparatus made it almost impossible for Western intelligence agencies to cultivate local intelligence sources.[6] The distance and isolation of the Soviet Union from the United States also meant that American intelligence agencies needed access to listening posts in the Arctic, Asia, and Europe, and the current and former British colonies were very useful for this purpose. The British Isles themselves were well located to monitor communications in the western Soviet Union and Eastern Europe, and signals intelligence stations in Cyprus, Ceylon (now Sri Lanka), Hong Kong, Singapore, and elsewhere allowed GCHQ good coverage of much of the rest of the So-viet bloc. Although some of Britain's former colonies, such as Sri Lanka, were unwilling to allow the United States to build signals intelligence facilities on their territory, they did permit Britain to build or continue to operate such facilities. Often their true purpose was hidden from the public (and perhaps from the host governments) by describing them as "communications relay facilities."[7] Britain also was able to use these territories to engage in aerial surveillance and intelligence collection during the early cold war, when the State Department blocked similar flights by the American military.[8] Britain's geographic location and experience of empire also gave the Royal Navy useful capabilities for ocean surveillance of the eastern Mediterranean, the Indian Ocean, and the North Sea, all areas of strategic importance during the cold war and regions in which the U.S. Navy lacked effective reconnaissance capabilities.[9] By 1951 the United States had established at least seven listening posts in Britain or British-controlled territories and was relying heavily on GCHQ for intercepting signals from the Soviet Union and other targets of interest.[10]

Britain's third asset was a large and experienced intelligence apparatus. Although American intelligence agencies in the early cold war period were much bigger and better funded than their British counterparts, the British nonetheless could contribute in important ways. American signals intelligence therefore continued to rely heavily on GCHQ for coverage of military and diplomatic signals traffic in Eastern Europe, as well as in the Middle East and Africa, regions where the United States had few such resources.[11]

These British capabilities were reflected in American thinking about postwar cooperation. For example, even though the U.S. Joint Intelligence Committee (JIC) stopped sending intelligence reports to the British at the end of the war in the Pacific in August 1945, the British continued to send their reports to their American counterparts in hopes of continuing their sharing of intelligence. By September 1946 the JIC decided that

> IF it is desired to continue to receive the British JIC intelligence estimates it is submitted that it must be done on an exchange basis, otherwise the source will dry up. Since there are many areas, particularly in parts of Europe, the Near East and the Middle East, where the British sources of information are superior to those of the United States, it is believed desirable that the United States JIC continue to receive such estimates.[12]

American intelligence officials were also in a good position to evaluate the accuracy of British intelligence capabilities. The close wartime cooperation between the two countries' intelligence services meant that the Americans had direct knowledge of the extent of Britain's resources for gathering and analyzing intelligence, as many of them had been developed jointly by the two countries during the war.

Incentives to Defect

American and British interests in European security were very closely aligned after 1947, giving the British government few incentives to violate its sharing agreements with the United States. Before this time, the American government had hoped to cooperate with the Soviet Union and to minimize its direct commitment to European security. British decision makers, in contrast, repeatedly called for a stronger American commitment to European security. The governments of both Winston Churchill and Clement Atlee urged the United States to take a harder line toward the Soviet Union, viewing it as the principal threat to European security after the war. But American decision makers initially disagreed with this assessment, believing instead that continued cooperation with the Soviet Union still was possible. After the termination of hostilities against Japan, President Harry Truman had moved quickly to distance the United States from its British ally, abruptly ending the wartime lend-lease program and quickly winding down the combined boards that coordinated the Anglo-American war effort, in part to avoid "conveying the impression that London and Washington were 'ganging up' on Russia."[13] In his famous "Iron Curtain" speech attended by President Truman in 1946, the former British prime minister, Winston Churchill, advocated an alliance of the United States, Britain, and other countries against the Soviet Union. But Truman publicly distanced himself from Churchill's remarks. Although British ministers and officials continued to believe that an alliance would be valuable, they largely dropped the issue because of American disinterest.

The original American approach left much of the responsibility for European security to cooperation between Britain and the Soviet Union, with the United States playing a supporting role on the Continent and a dominant role in the Western Hemisphere.[14] Roosevelt opposed maintaining a sizable American force in Europe or formally committing the

United States to maintaining security on the Continent, and Truman largely continued this policy after Roosevelt's death in 1945.[15] American military planners feared an alliance would divert resources from the development of new weapons such as atomic bombs and missiles. But the most important reason was that American officials held out the hope that they could reach a comprehensive settlement with the Soviet Union on the security of Europe.

During 1946 and especially in 1947, the United States finally came to see Soviet-inspired subversion as the main threat to Western Europe's security. The failure of its policy of attempting to cooperate with the Soviet Union led the United States to devote more attention to countering the appeals of Communist parties in Western Europe by implementing the Truman Doctrine and Marshall Plan and encouraging the political integration of Western Europe.[16]

The final break with the Soviets came at the London conference of foreign ministers in December 1947. The British and Americans held out little hope that the meeting would result in success, an expectation that proved correct when the meeting collapsed without any agreements or decisions to reconvene. The British, Americans, and (more reluctantly) French responded in December 1947 and January 1948 by moving toward the creation of a West German state.[17] Shortly afterward, the British foreign secretary, Ernest Bevin, proposed to Marshall that "we must devise some western democratic system comprising the Americans, ourselves, France, Italy, etc., and of course the Dominions. This would not be a formal alliance, but an understanding backed by power, money and resolute action." Bevin emphasized the effect that such an arrangement would have on the French government, which was concerned about both the activities of the French Communist Party and the steps being taken by the Americans and British to create a West German government. Bevin's idea of a "Western Union" would help resolve these problems by creating "confidence in Western Europe that further Communist inroads would be stopped" and by using the United States to ensure that a reconstituted German government would not pose a threat to its neighbors. Secretary of State George Marshall did not reject the proposal outright, as American decision makers had in the recent past, but instead expressed interest and instructed his department to seek additional information from its British counterpart.[18] Over the next four months the United States, Canada, and Britain negotiated, first secretly among themselves and then with a larger group of European countries, what became the North Atlantic Treaty that committed the United States to defend Western Europe.[19]

By 1947 American officials thus had few doubts that postwar Britain shared their fundamental security policy interests. A report on this question prepared by the CIA concluded that "while the UK has differed occasionally with the US in the emphases on and approach to the German problem, the UK Government was and is in fundamental agreement with that of the US. . . . [T]here has never been any doubt about British disposition to resist Communist expansion."[20] Indeed, over the preceding two years the United States had adopted most of the policies that the Churchill and Atlee governments had pressed on it since 1945. While the two countries did have conflicting interests over some nonsecurity issues, such as international trade and the pace of decolonization, by 1947 their European security and other policies toward the Soviet Union were closely in line with each other. Britain and the United States worked together on all the major questions of European security, including the decision to create a west German state, the negotiation of the North Atlantic Treaty, the permanent deployment of American forces in Europe (including the basing of aircraft armed with nuclear weapons in Britain), and German rearmament in the early 1950s.

In the late 1940s and early 1950s Britain was considered trustworthy in regard to both its internal security and its foreign policy interests. Britain was viewed as much more politically reliable than either France or West Germany. Unlike France, Britain did not have a large and politically influential Communist party. Instead, its Communist party was a marginal force outside the mainstream political competition and was never likely to participate in government and gain access to secrets that it might then pass on to the Soviet Union.[21] While American documents from the period are full of doubts about the political reliability of the postwar French and West German governments, they show remarkably little doubt about Britain on this score.

The CIA concluded that Britain would solidly back the United States on all major issues of European security, although domestic opposition might lead the government to occasionally pursue an independent line on secondary issues.[22] Rear Admiral Tom Inglis, chief of naval intelligence, did argue in October 1947 that the United States should be wary about continuing to share intelligence, insisting that Britain was unreliable because the government would pass scientific intelligence on to

British firms, might share American intelligence with other members of the Commonwealth, and because senior members of the Labour government were "socialists."[23] But Inglis seems to have been the only senior American official to express such concerns; his air force counterpart replied to his worries that Anglo-American cooperation on intelligence was more important and valuable to his service than was collaboration with the U.S. Navy.[24] American officials did not worry a great deal about the possibility that the British government had been penetrated by the intelligence services of Soviet Union. In fact, some individuals in the British civil service and scientific establishment did pass important secrets to the Soviet Union during the 1940s. They included scientists who had collaborated on the atomic bomb during the Second World War, the first secretary of the British embassy in Washington and later head of the Foreign Office's American section, and a liaison officer between British and American intelligence stationed in Washington in the late 1940s. These individuals gave to the Soviet Union important details of the American atomic weapons program, American and British strategies and perceptions of the Soviet Union, and information about intelligence operations directed against the Soviet bloc.[25]

Outcomes

The United States shared more intelligence with Britain than with any other European country in the years after the Second World War. To govern much of this sharing, American and British officials negotiated a series of agreements and memoranda, known collectively as the UKUSA agreement. The structures created by UKUSA were largely anarchic, giving both states roughly equal rights and responsibilities.

As early as June 1945 American military officers agreed to continue their wartime signals intelligence cooperation with the British, which would now be directed against the Soviet Union.[26] Three months later, the secretary of war, the secretary of the navy, and the secretary of state wrote Truman that during the Second World War the United States and Britain "collaborated closely in regard to cryptanalytic techniques and procedures and exchanged fully the intelligence derived from cryptanalysis. The results of this collaboration were very profitable." They advised the president that "in view of the disturbed conditions of the world and the necessity of keeping informed of technical developments and possible hostile intentions of foreign nations [two lines redacted] it is recommended that you authorise continuation of collaboration between the United States and the United Kingdom in the field of communications intelligence." Truman agreed, and within weeks, detailed negotiations opened in Washington. These talks were concluded in London in early 1946, producing a (still classified) agreement. Additional negotiations over the next two years dealt with remaining issues, such as the reorganization of the Commonwealth, and resulted in the UKUSA agreement by June 1948.[27]

While the UKUSA accord remains classified, it is widely believed to follow closely the declassified 1943 BRUSA agreement between the United States and Britain on wartime intelligence sharing.[28] It is known that the UKUSA agreement is a tiered arrangement in which intelligence sharing between the United States and Britain (along with Canada and Australia) usually is closer than with the other countries that joined later. The agreement established common security procedures and standardized technical terms, code words, and training across the participating countries' intelligence services, ensuring that shared intelligence was handled consistently and was not likely to be misinterpreted by the receiving state. The agreement assigned each party a region of the world to cover. Initially, Britain was responsible for Africa and the Soviet Union west of the Urals; Canada covered the northern Soviet Union; and the United States assumed responsibility for the rest of the world. Although sharing among the partners was widespread, it was based on the "need to know" principle: in general, governments chose not to share intelligence if it concerned only bilateral or commercial issues, dealt with sensitive counterintelligence information, or had been obtained from a third state.[29] In addition to their close collaboration on signals intelligence, the United States and Britain together managed a network for ocean surveillance and monitored foreign radio broadcasts.[30] The two countries apparently also agreed not to engage in covert political operations against each other or to recruit agents from the other country's nationals,[31] although it is not clear if these limits also prevented each party from monitoring the other's communications.

The Anglo-American intelligence-sharing relationship was less hierarchical than that between the United States and West Germany. The reason for this was that the American authorities judged that the similar foreign policy interests of the two countries, and the absence of a powerful domestic Communist movement, made Britain less likely to renege on the agreement. The United States thus saw less need to invest in a hierarchical relationship to prevent Britain's defection. Note, however, that hierarchy was not entirely absent even from this relationship between very close allies. Although these hierarchical elements provided some defenses against defection, perhaps more important, they addressed distributional concerns. The agreement's rules about how widely a receiving state could disseminate shared intelligence within its government, its common security procedures, and limits on what intelligence would be shared enabled the United States, for example, to monitor how securely Britain treated the shared intelligence, thereby providing one check against defection. The basing of substantial numbers of American personnel in Britain and in British-controlled territories to staff collection apparatuses and to work at the technical level with their British counterparts ensured direct American access to most raw signals intelligence collection, meaning that the United States was less reliant on British analysis.

At the same time, the rules and practices of the UKUSA agreement also placed some potentially costly limits on American behavior. That is, the rules regarding the internal dissemination of intelligence also applied to the United States and thus gave Britain some reassurance that shared intelligence would not be leaked to Soviet agents in the United States. The expectation that the participating governments would share most of the intelligence offered far more benefits to Britain than to the United States, since it gave the former access to much of the intelligence collected by the latter's far larger and better-financed intelligence agencies. These provisions also created a clearly articulated expectation about what sort of behavior did and did not violate the agreement. American attempts to withhold intelligence from Britain would be a clear signal that the dominant power was intent on managing the relationship in a way that ignored important British interests. And the fact that many of the technical intelligence collection facilities were jointly staffed by American and British personnel and were located in Britain or in British-controlled territory could give the British government leverage in the relationship. Britain could have retaliated against American defection by restricting American access to such facilities. Furthermore, the UKUSA agreement was based on the principle of regional specialization, with each country covering an important part of the world and thereby relieving their partner of collecting this intelligence. Specialization also provided the weaker partner, Britain, with some leverage against American defection, since it could then retaliate by withholding intelligence collected from its assigned region of the world.

These elements of hierarchy were more important to addressing some of the concerns that each country had about the distribution of the costs and benefits of cooperation. UKUSA was an expensive and technologically challenging undertaking. It involved the creation and maintenance of a global network of monitoring facilities and the capacity to store, analyze, and disseminate the huge amounts of raw information this network could collect. Britain's smaller and less dynamic economy meant that it could not afford many of these expenses. But the United States could and so provided most of the manpower, money, and technological resources as the UKUSA agreement evolved. This willingness and ability to bear a larger share of the financial cost allowed the United States to secure Britain's participation in a venture that it likely would otherwise be unable to afford. Another way that hierarchy may have contributed to cooperation was in the establishment and updating of technical standards for intelligence collection, internal security, and counterintelligence. Many of these standards likely adhered more closely to those already in place in the United States, whose government agencies and private firms have been important to the development of new technologies to collect communications intelligence.[32] This meant that Britain had to adopt to American practices while the United States could continue to implement its existing standards, thus partially offsetting its larger financial contribution.

In the early 1950s the United States discovered that some British officials and scientists had passed important secrets to the Soviet Union, but this does not seem to have seriously eroded the United States' trust in Britain or to have hurt subsequent Anglo-American intelligence sharing. The reason is that American officials did not view this as strictly a "British" problem. Instead, they concluded that the Soviet Union had managed to penetrate both the United States and Britain, as well as Canada, with roughly equal success in the 1930s and 1940s. The U.S. government was intensely concerned with detecting agents of foreign governments within its own apparatus and viewed similar penetrations in other countries whose political systems and foreign policy interests were largely aligned with its own as normal, understandable, or unavoidable, although in retrospect it appears that the British government delayed informing the United States of this espionage out of the concern that doing so would damage intelligence and nuclear cooperation between the two countries.[33]

When informed by the Canadian prime minister in September 1945 that Canada had information about Soviet espionage in Britain and Canada that likely included American officials, President Truman responded that such activities "would not be surprising" and that "there must be similar penetrations by the Russians into the conditions in the United States."[34] American counterintelligence officials assumed that the Soviet espionage included interconnected networks of agents in all three countries.[35] A reasonable response would have been to monitor more closely the loyalty of the participating countries' senior officials. It is not clear whether this occurred, as few documents on the functioning of the UKUSA agreement after the mid-1950s have been declassified.

Intelligence sharing between Britain and the United States also survived the Suez crisis of 1956, the one time when the two countries' security policies were seriously at odds. In late 1956 Britain, France, and Israel agreed, without directly informing the United States, on a plan to invade Egypt and overthrow the Gamal Abdel Nasser regime. Each had different but overlapping reasons for wanting to remove Nasser. Britain feared his control over the Suez Canal, an important avenue for British trade; the French resented his support for the independence movement in their colony of Algeria; and Israel saw his Arab nationalist regime as a threat to its security.[36] The United States strongly opposed its allies' military intervention in Egypt by refusing economic assistance to Britain and using movements of the American fleet in the Mediterranean to interfere with British and French naval activities supporting the invasion. But the United States and Britain were able to restore their political relationship shortly after the British withdrew from the conflict. American leaders concluded that preserving the political cohesion of NATO outweighed the importance of continuing to punish Britain. American intelligence officials also saw that the interests of the United States and Britain in the Middle East remained compatible after this episode, and the two countries' intelligence services continued to share intelligence on the region and to engage in coordinated covert operations.[37]

The United States had much to gain from sharing intelligence with Britain, which could provide signals intelligence and ocean reconnaissance from around the world and had a strong record of intelligence analysis. American officials after 1946 saw Britain as having foreign policy interests that closely mirrored their own and no domestic Communist movement of any consequence. Britain therefore had few reasons to defect. This combination of mutual benefits and convergent interests explains why the two countries were able to negotiate an intelligence-sharing agreement that placed few hierarchic constraints on each other's actions. From the American perspective, there seemed little need to develop an elaborate and costly hierarchy to oversee British compliance with the UKUSA agreements. Anarchic sharing, in which each state decided how to implement the agreement, was an adequate solution.

This analysis sheds new light on important aspects of Anglo-American intelligence cooperation. Many argue that the wide sharing of sensitive intelligence on a roughly equal basis between the United States and Britain is, to a considerable degree, motivated solely by the two countries' common foreign policy interests or by their intelligence agencies' wartime collaboration and common organizational cultures. But these approaches predict far less hierarchy than the Anglo-American sharing arrangements actually contained. Britain's and the United States' similar foreign policy interests were important because they reduced the incentives on both sides to defect, but they did not eliminate them entirely. Available analyses of the Anglo-American intelligence relationship do not devote much attention to this and therefore cannot explain why both the United States and Britain could benefit from some hierarchy in their relationship. Others hold that the close relationship between American and British intelligence agencies during the Second World War, and the important role of British intelligence in teaching their American counterparts about intelligence collection and analysis, may have made American officials and agencies lean toward cooperation with their British colleagues.

Verne Newton, for example, holds that this history of close collaboration made it difficult for American intelligence officials to believe that the Soviets' penetration of Britain could be very deep or further compromise important secrets. Once it had been revealed in the 1950s that this trust had been abused by at least a handful of British officials, American intelligence and counterintelligence agencies tried to minimize the perception of the damage, which reflected poorly on their earlier decisions to collaborate so closely with the British.[38] But if American intelligence officials were willing to overlook or to excuse defection in this way, it seems unlikely that they would have built into the UKUSA agreement any monitoring and enforcement provisions. Furthermore, nearly identical policy interests or close organizational ties cannot explain successful intelligence sharing by the United States with other states, such as West Germany, that did not share these characteristics.

FRANCE

Benefits of Sharing Intelligence

In the eyes of American decision makers, French foreign intelligence had relatively little to contribute. The locations where France had signals intelligence listening posts—metropolitan France, West and North Africa, and Vietnam—were not particularly useful for monitoring Soviet bloc communications. Much of the French intelligence establishment's effort was focused on anticolonial movements in Algeria and Vietnam, rather than the United States' priority target of the Soviet Union.[39] French intelligence agencies also were much smaller and less capable than comparable British organizations. The French civilian intelligence service had only about fifteen hundred employees. While the British and Americans had invested huge sums in developing technical means of collecting intelligence during the war, the French had been unable to do so, and it was not clear if they could catch up with their allies. Like their Western counterparts, the French relied on interrogating refugees and defectors from Soviet-controlled territory as their main human intelligence source. But geography put France (and Britain) at a disadvantage on this score, as most of the people moving westward were recruited by the new West German intelligence service.[40] The French intelligence services also spread their resources and experience too thinly by trying to provide global coverage, rather than concentrating their resources on the Soviet Union or some other threat.[41]

Incentives to Defect

American officials had serious doubts about whether they could trust postwar French governments to share intelligence reliably. This distrust was the result of important differences in the two countries' foreign policy interests and concerns about Communist influence in France.

One early and persistent source of apprehension was that the French government's foreign policy interests, particularly concerning the future status of Germany, differed substantially from those of the United States. Although for the United States preventing the rise of an unstable or aggressive Germany after the Second World War was an important priority, for France, it was vital. French leaders feared Germany's economic and political reconstruction and advocated very restrictive international controls over the postwar German polity that would prevent it from threatening France in the future. American leaders, however, felt that a more rapid economic and political rehabilitation of West Germany would reduce the costs of occupation, spur economic growth in Europe, and eventually allow the German military to contribute to the NATO alliance. French governments were forced to recognize that they lacked the power to impose their preferred solutions to the German problem and reluctantly acquiesced to American and British plans for the country.

As early as 1944, French objectives for Germany included either detaching or maintaining international control over the politically and economically important western regions of the Ruhr, Saar, and Rhineland; suppressing German industry that could contribute to military production; preventing the creation of German military forces; and forcing Germany to pay large reparations. But the American and British governments did not share these goals and used their occupation of most of West Germany to block French designs. The French also were not invited to the Potsdam Conference on the future of Germany, held in the summer of 1945, at which the United States, Britain, and the Soviet Union decided, contrary to the French position, to begin establishing German government departments under the occupying powers' control and to demand reparations only if doing so left "enough resources to enable the German people to subsist without external assistance."[42] In 1946, the French refused to participate in the Anglo-American decision to combine their zones of occupation, fearing that doing so would remove their most important source of leverage in future negotiations over the status of Germany. This provoked the American secretary of state to publicly oppose the idea of partitioning West Germany, as the French proposed.[43] The French government then relented in 1947, instead advocating international control over the industrial resources of the Ruhr and agreeing in principle to merge the French occupation zone with the Anglo-American zones.

This change in policy did not reflect a rethinking of French interests but was largely dictated by France's desire to accept the American offer of Marshall Plan assistance.[44] In addition, in 1948 the French acquiesced to the creation of a West German state not because it would best guarantee their security but because they realized that the British and Americans would insist on it and could achieve it despite French objections. French policy thus shifted from obstruction to cooperation in an attempt to extract as many concessions as possible from the Americans, including international control over the German economy, a commitment to European security through NATO, and, by 1950, international control over West Germany's economic development through the creation of the European Coal and Steel Community.[45]

For their part, American foreign policy officials worried about the political influence of the Parti communiste français (PCF) and whether party members or sympathizers might pass on to the Soviet Union any intelligence provided by the United States. American officials believed that the PCF, which had played an important role in resisting the Nazis and had participated in early postwar coalition governments, was trying to place its supporters in important positions in the army, police, intelligence agencies, and government ministries.[46]

The CIA viewed the PCF as "the instrument of the Kremlin in France" and surmised that it received significant funding from the Soviet Union.[47] These concerns received attention at the highest levels, and American government officials closely monitored the French government's attempts to remove Communists from positions of influence.[48] American officials further feared that influential French Communists would obtain and pass on to the Soviet Union the results of confidential negotiations among the Western powers.[49] In the late 1940s, numerous revelations surfaced that seemed to confirm this view; for example, the chief of security of France's Air Ministry was arrested for passing secret information to a Yugoslav military attaché; France's director of scientific research, who had access to the French atomic energy agency, was suspected of being a Communist; and a former member of the Communist resistance who joined the army after the war was arrested in 1949 for passing technical documents from the Toulon arsenal to the Soviet Union.[50]

Concerns about French internal security clearly influenced the American's willingness to share intelligence. The U.S. Air Force intelligence agency, for example, announced in 1948 that

any staff talks that may be held with France can be considered secure only if information is issued for the personal use of the officers concerned and may be delivered orally by them only to their immediate supervisors provided it can be guaranteed those supervisors are not Communist or fellow travelers.[51]

The U.S. Army's concerns about Communist influence led it to refuse to share new weapons designs with the French, even though this forced the French to develop weapons on their own and slowed the pace of French rearmament, an important priority for the United States.[52] This concern with French security extended well beyond intelligence sharing into traditional diplomatic relations. The British and Americans decided on the creation of West Germany before discussing the issue with the French.[53] Two participants in the crucial early discussions among the United States, Britain, and Canada on the creation of NATO noted that France was deliberately excluded from the talks because it was feared that otherwise their content would be communicated to the Soviet Union.[54] American officials believed that France was a "security risk" and would quickly leak details to the Soviet Union.[55]

Outcomes

In the early cold war period, the United States and France shared little intelligence. They did share some information because it ended in the early 1960s, when the United States stopped sharing signals intelligence with France because of unspecified "security considerations" and President Charles de Gaulle ordered the French intelligence service to end its contacts with the CIA.[56] But the sharing that did take place before this was not governed by an arrangement as detailed or open as the UKUSA agreement. Although France (as well as some other NATO members) became recognized "third parties" to the UKUSA agreement, the Americans and British were far less likely to share intelligence with these countries.[57] Indeed, the Americans and British seemed to have taken steps *not* to share intelligence with the French. This problem arose in the context of the NATO alliance, whose effective military functioning in war depended on accurate intelligence about the Soviet order of battle. The American and British militaries considered full intelligence sharing through NATO to be insecure, even though during the early cold war period NATO's military headquarters was staffed by only American, British, and French officers. Instead, American army intelligence informally joined GCHQ to supply relevant intelligence that would be used only by British and American, not French, officers at NATO headquarters.[58]

Compared with Britain or West Germany, in the early cold war period, France had little foreign intelligence that was of value to the United States. It could provide some valuable intelligence on domestic French developments, especially those concerning the PCF's activities. American officials also concluded that France's position on West Germany, as well as the PCF's influence, created motives to defect, by either withholding relevant intelligence or passing on shared intelligence to third parties. The United States did not consider creating a hierarchical relationship to reduce French incentives to defect because it would have cost more to the United States than the intelligence was worth. The French government would have demanded that the United States limit West Germany's rehabilitation in exchange for suppressing the PCF. But the United States would have been unwilling to do so because the reintegration of Germany was the linchpin of American policy toward Europe.

West Germany

Benefits of Sharing Intelligence

What became West Germany had two assets that made its intelligence useful to the United States. First, a key American intelligence priority was information about Soviet military activities in its occupied zone and throughout Eastern Europe.[59] West Germany's position on the front line of the East–West confrontation meant that listening posts on its territory were ideally positioned to monitor emissions from Warsaw Pact military forces in East Germany and Czechoslovakia. Signals intelligence stations in West Germany also were able to monitor communications deeper in the Soviet hinterland than were stations located elsewhere in Europe. As early as 1946 the U.S. Army's Counterintelligence Corps enlisted former German military officers with experience in signals intelligence on the eastern front and put them to work in listening posts. By 1948 the U.S. Army was building a signals direction-finding network across West Germany. West German signals intelligence operations provided valuable intelligence on Soviet air force activities during the Berlin airlift of 1948. James Critchfield, the CIA official who in 1948 recommended that the agency take over the German intelligence operations from the army, wrote that this was West Germany's most valuable contribution to American intelligence.[60] The army transferred these signals intelligence capabilities to German control in 1952 and continued to finance their operations for another four years.[61]

Second, significant human intelligence was available in West Germany. Of the millions of refugees and defectors who moved west during this period, some had valuable information about the Soviet bloc's military and scientific capabilities. West German officials interrogated many refugees and, later, defectors from the Soviet occupied zone. In addition, many former German army intelligence officers had had wartime experience in what was now Soviet-controlled territory. In 1946, a group of these officers, led by Reinhard Gehlen, the former head of the German Army's eastern front intelligence agency, began reconstituting their intelligence operations under the supervision of the U.S. Army in order to supply the United States with intelligence. The Gehlen Organization, as it was known, initially prepared reports for the United States on the Soviet military based on these officers' wartime experience. This information was particularly valuable, as the United States had little basic information about the Soviet military. The Gehlen Organization also interrogated thousands of individuals from Eastern Europe at displaced persons' camps in West Germany, thereby providing the United States with one of its only large-scale sources of immediate intelligence about the Soviet Union. Later the organization operated most of West Germany's signals intelligence listening posts and began recruiting networks of agents throughout Eastern Europe. The organization's networks in East Germany provided the most valuable intelligence to the United States.[62]

Incentives to Defect

American intelligence authorities valued the intelligence supplied by the Gehlen Organization but regularly questioned how much they could trust their West German collaborators. The most immediate issue was the background of the Gehlen Organization's members. Some had been members of the Nazi Party, and in 1946 some American military intelligence officials went on the record as opposing collaboration with the organization, fearing that the loyalty of many of its staff was questionable or could be subject to blackmail. The American in charge of overseeing the organization's activities during this period demanded that Gehlen release to him the names of all his employees and, furthermore, declared in his memoirs, which are largely positive about the Gehlen Organization, that he never entirely trusted the information that Gehlen gave him about the organization's personnel and activities.[63]

The Americans also were concerned that the organization in particular, as well as much of the rest of the West German government in general, had been penetrated by Soviet bloc intelligence services. For this reason, the army's Counterintelligence Corps in Germany mounted a large-scale operation to identify Communists in West Germany and warned the CIA, which by this time was responsible for the Gehlen Organization, that it should try to strengthen the security of its German counterpart.[64]

The second American worry concerned West German foreign policy, as well as the influence of the German Communist Party. Most American observers concluded that the party was weak and did not have enough support to seriously challenge West Germany's other parties, although there was some apprehension that the party could be used to organize sabotage and encourage violent political demonstrations.[65]

Of greater concern to the Americans was the emergence of nationalist opposition to the decision to divide Germany. An immediate problem was the Sozialistische Reichspartei, a neo-Nazi party that opposed division and achieved some electoral success before being outlawed. But the American concern with a future West German government's foreign policy went well beyond this single party. John McCloy, the U.S. high commissioner for West Germany, wrote to Washington as late as 1951 that

> most of the established political parties have also been stockpiling the merchandise of nationalism. . . . They seek to draw the followers of the extreme rightist forces or to prevent losses of their own, by attempting to appear as nationalistic as the extremists. . . . The consequences of such a course, if long continued, must be general disaster.[66]

Even the pro-American government of Konrad Adenauer and his party, the Christian Democratic Union, which supported the decision to divide Germany but also called for unification free of Soviet domination, occasionally seemed suspect on this score. A CIA report in 1949 noted that "the proposed new German Government is still an unknown and untested entity with many points of disagreement, real and potential, between German leaders and the occupation authorities,"[67] while another report observed that "few Germans, given the opportunity, would hesitate to play off the US against the USSR in an endeavor to achieve unification on their own terms."[68]

More than a year later the CIA still was worrying about West Germany's adherence to American policy, fretting that

> German national aspirations are not likely to be realized in sufficient degree and in sufficient time to justify in German eyes a pro-western policy which would exclude a modus vivendi with the East. . . . Powerful political forces, both those supporting and those opposing the Government, will seek a position of neutrality between East and West.[69]

Adenauer and many other West German politicians initially complained that the plans for creating a west German state while occupation troops remained in the country indefinitely would burden them with the responsibility of supporting policies over which they did not have full control.[70] Adenauer appealed for political support to German refugee groups, some of which attached particular importance to unification, and as late as 1952 American officials worried (incorrectly, it turned out) that Adenauer might be tempted to back a Soviet offer of German unification on the condition that Germany not ally with any other state.[71] The leadership of the Social Democratic Party, the other large political party in West Germany, also consistently criticized the creation of a west German state as a barrier to full German reunification.[72] Like Adenauer's Christian Democratic Union, the Social Democrats hoped to appeal for political support to refugees from the Soviet zone and former German territories in Eastern Europe.[73]

Outcomes

Although American officials valued the intelligence on the Soviet bloc that West Germany could provide, they worried that the government could not be trusted with shared intelligence. This combination of valuable intelligence but an unreliable intelligence service and government led the Americans to insist on direct control of all intelligence operations conducted by the Gehlen Organization, even after the creation of the West German state in 1949.

Before this date, U.S. Army intelligence and then the CIA ran the Gehlen Organization directly. They financed the organization's activities and based American staff permanently in the organization's headquarters to oversee its daily activities, monitor its expenditures, and receive intelligence reports.[74] In part, this direct supervision was dictated by the Americans' unwillingness to trust the organization to operate independently, for fear that it might serve as a base for former Nazi officials or for penetration by the Soviet Union and its clients. But this sort of arrangement was not unusual during the occupation, when American civilian and military authorities were organizing and directing the new West German central government organs.

The creation of the Federal Republic in 1949 naturally raised questions about whether and how control over the Gehlen Organization should be transferred to the new West German government. In the end, while most other government bureaus were transferred to German control, the Gehlen Organization was not. The CIA and the army, both of which dealt with the Gehlen Organization during this period, maintained that security problems made such a transfer too risky. After a thorough analysis of the organization, the CIA concluded that it was providing quite valuable intelligence to the United States, especially on developments in the Soviet zone.[75] Yet there also were serious concerns about whether Gehlen and his colleagues shared the same goals as the Americans. James Critchfield, the CIA official responsible for investigating the organization, later wrote rather diplomatically that

> I had personally observed that the Gehlen Organization was providing the high quality and real-time intelligence of Soviet air activity in East Germany. Considering the circumstances I wondered why the United States was even considering drastic action on the Gehlen Organization. Also, it seemed to me that . . . politically the United States had passed the point of no return in forming a West German state, a factor the CIA would have to take into consideration in shaping a plan for the ultimate disposition of the Gehlen Organization. . . . I consciously avoided any effort to sort out my own assessment of Gehlen as

an individual beyond the fact that he was the dominant figure . . . and at times could be difficult.[76]

Elsewhere Critchfield noted that while the organization produced intelligence on the Soviet bloc that was as good or better that that produced by the Western powers, he also observed that "life with the CIA would have been much easier for Gehlen had mutual trust been an element of the relationship from the start."[77]

The CIA decided to reduce its direct control over the Gehlen Organization only modestly. Under the new division of responsibilities, the CIA would retain responsibility for developing intelligence requirements, and the organization would collect and analyze the intelligence. The Americans insisted on retaining the practice of attaching CIA personnel to each of the organization's departments, receiving all the organization's intelligence reports and evaluations, and disclosing the identity of the organization's personnel.[78] This last demand led to particular friction between the Americans and Gehlen. The Americans worried that in his drive to rebuild a German intelligence service, Gehlen might hire military or intelligence personnel with close connections to the Nazi regime. Doing so would give the Soviet Union a public relations coup. It might also threaten the security of the Gehlen Organization if individuals could be blackmailed to betray its security under threat that their past associations with the Nazi Party might be exposed.[79]

The CIA and, before it, the U.S. Army also restricted the targets of Gehlen's intelligence collection activities, refusing to allow the organization to collect intelligence in West Germany and limiting its overseas counterintelligence activities. Upon taking over its liaison responsibilities, the CIA insisted on closer management of the organization's activities in East Germany and decided to approve operations in other areas of Soviet influence on a case-by-case basis, which constituted a large share of the organization's activities. These stipulations were explicitly intended to "give us a degree of control and an insight into their operations which has been non-existent in the past."[80] Gehlen urged throughout the early 1950s that his organization become part of the West German state with continued CIA funding, but the agency decided to continue its more active and direct monitoring.[81] This arrangement lasted until shortly after West Germany's admission to NATO in 1955, when the Gehlen Organization became independent of American control and was transformed into the West German intelligence service, the Bundesnachrichtendienst (BND).

In exchange for its control of German intelligence activities, the United States provided West Germany with considerable benefits. The intelligence-sharing arrangement was part of the larger American–German political and security relationship, in which West Germany effectively agreed to limit its freedom of action in the area of security policy in exchange for American support for the creation of the Federal Republic. The United States financed much of the Gehlen Organization's activities and paid for the construction of listening posts along the intra-German border, seeing such investments as a good intelligence value. The West German government, whose priority was to rebuild an economy devastated by war, would have had to spend a substantial amount of money to develop these facilities if the Americans had not.[82]

The United States also did not actively press the West German government to remove supporters of the former Nazi regime from the country's intelligence services. Indeed, by the early 1950s the United States ceased to insist on making sure that the West German intelligence agency did not hire former Nazi war criminals, and as a result, dozens of the Gehlen Organization's staff were former SD or Gestapo officers.[83] The Americans' most important concession was to collaborate with German intelligence in the first place. Permitting West Germany to develop its own intelligence apparatus, even one with the hierarchical controls created by the Americans, did expose the United States to the possibility that it could defect.

American officials valued West Germany's contribution in the areas of signals intelligence, especially tactical military signals intelligence; its interrogation of refugees and defectors; its general knowledge of Soviet infrastructure, military systems, and doctrines; and human intelligence from Soviet-controlled East Germany. The evidence is clear that Americans in many agencies worried about the extent to which they could trust the Gehlen Organization and the West German government. Their mistrust was driven by concerns about the political orientations of the Gehlen Organization's members, their susceptibility to blackmail because of their past support of Nazi rule, potential popular support for the anti-

American Communist and right-wing parties, and the possibility that the Adenauer government would accede to Soviet proposals for a reunified but neutral Germany. American authorities attempted to capture the benefits of sharing intelligence by carefully structuring their relationship with the Germans. This included reserving authority over the Gehlen's Organization's intelligence requirements and priorities, controlling its activities by supplying the budget and demanding regular accountings for expenditures, engaging in counterintelligence by disclosing to the CIA the identities and past activities of the organization's staff, and secretly monitoring the organization's activities. The Americans' crucial innovation here was their insistence on a hierarchical relationship with their German counterparts. This allowed the Americans to know whether their partner was acting in a manner consistent with U.S. interests and fully sharing relevant intelligence. Directly controlling many of the German intelligence services' collection priorities and practices ensured that they were focusing on targets of concern to the United States; counterintelligence activities were designed to prevent reneging by disloyal German employees or agents; and requirements for financial controls and accounting allowed the Americans to track the true activities of the German service and enabled them to threaten to withdraw or reduce their funding.

The United States also reassured West Germany that it would not break its promise to share intelligence. Most important here was its decision to rely on the Germans in the first place, when the United States could have developed its own intelligence apparatus in the country. Simply sharing intelligence gave the Germans some leverage over their more powerful partner, which ran not an insignificant risk that German officials would pass secrets to the Soviet bloc and exposed the United States to criticism for collaborating and even rehabilitating former supporters of the Nazi regime. Finally, the hierarchical elements in the relationship also addressed bargaining differences between the two countries. Hierarchy allowed the United States to dictate the West Germans' intelligence collection standards, making sure that the shared intelligence could be more easily incorporated into American intelligence estimates. The United States also was willing to finance most of the development and many of the operating expenses of the West German intelligence service, at a time when the West German government would have had difficulty funding it.

Conclusions

What do these case studies say about the ability of states to form mutually beneficial intelligence-sharing arrangements under the threat of defection by their partners? How well does the relational contracting theory of intelligence sharing compare with the alternative explanations introduced in the previous chapter? The failure to share much intelligence with France is consistent with relational contracting as well as the trust and neoliberal institutionalist explanations of cooperation. All three theories agree that concerns about defection may lead states to refrain from cooperation. This is precisely what occurred in the French case: American officials felt that France did not have a great deal of valuable intelligence to share and that they had strong motives to defect. Consistent with all three explanations, the absence of large gains scuttled any serious effort by the United States to share intelligence with France.

The value of relational contracting becomes clear when comparing the French and German cases. Explanations of cooperation based on mutual trust or of neoliberal institutionalism predict that concerns about German defection would lead to the same outcome that similar concerns produced for France. Although the United States did not share intelligence with France owing to concerns about defection, it overcame similar concerns to cooperate with West Germany through a hierarchical intelligence-sharing arrangement. A focus on mutual trust cannot explain this outcome, since there was little trust between the United States and West Germany in the area of intelligence sharing. Neoliberal institutionalism also has difficulty accounting for American–German sharing, since it assumes that international politics is anarchic and does not consider how states can construct a hierarchical relationship to overcome mistrust. The third expectation developed in chapter 1 does, however, provide an explanation for this outcome. American authorities attempted to capture the benefits of sharing by carefully structuring their relationship with the Germans to avoid the costs of defection. Process tracing indicates that the United States used many of the hierarchical mechanisms for monitoring and supervising subordinates. These included reserving authority for generating intelligence requirements and priorities, monitoring West Germany's compliance with its leadership by providing much of the funding and demanding regular accountings for expenditures, and effectively engaging in counterintelligence by disclosing to the CIA the identities and past activities of the organization's staff and by secretly monitoring the organization's activities. The Americans' crucial innovation was insisting on a hierarchical relationship with their German counterparts. Hierarchy was the most efficient way in which they could enlist German help in collecting and analyzing intelligence. It also was preferable to sharing through anarchic institutions, which would have placed few restraints on German incentives to defect. Furthermore, a hierarchy was a more attractive option than developing, at a considerable expense of money and time, a full-fledged American government intelligence apparatus in West Germany that would have duplicated the capabilities available to the Federal Republic. Hierarchy was preferable to direct intelligence collection and analysis because the partial autonomy granted to the Gehlen Organization persuaded the West German government and the leaders of the West German intelligence apparatus to see the substantial benefits of, and therefore to support, collaboration with the Americans.

American officials were less worried that their British counterparts would act in ways contrary to American interests. Consistent with the second expectation of relational contracting, they thus were willing to accept a less hierarchical intelligence-sharing arrangement, in which Britain was a more equal partner with the United States. Furthermore, the potential costs to the United States of British defection were mitigated by the fact that Britain's intelligence strengths and weaknesses overlapped with those of the United States. Again, process tracing provides information consistent with this interpretation. For example, American officials were less concerned about directly overseeing counterintelligence in Britain than they were in West Germany, even though they knew that the Soviet Union had highly placed agents in both countries' intelligence agencies. The reason was that the Americans viewed their own government as also vulnerable to penetration by the Soviet Union. The Soviets might obtain some of the same intelligence from its agents in Britain as it did from those in the United States. But the additional loss of security involved was more modest than in the case of West Germany, where a Soviet agent could derive equally valuable intelligence from a different source. Even in this case, however, the Americans were careful to structure the UKUSA agreement to reduce concerns about Britain's reneging.

These elements of hierarchy served both to reassure the United States about Britain's commitment to the relationship and to convince the

British that the Americans would not exploit their dominant position. The importance of hierarchy for underpinning and sustaining the Anglo-American intelligence relationship has been largely unrecognized by the existing research. The Americans' failure to reconsider this arrangement after the revelations of Soviet spying in Britain is more difficult to explain, although as discussed earlier, there is some evidence that the Americans viewed this as unrepresentative of Britain's overall foreign policy position.

Finally, the outcomes of these cases may simply reflect power imbalances between the three countries and the United States. Perhaps the United States preferred incorporating elements of hierarchy into *all* its intelligence-sharing relationships to counter incentives to opportunism. This conclusion would contradict the fourth expectation described in the previous chapter, that such power imbalances are a necessary but not a sufficient condition for creating an intelligence-sharing hierarchy. The American occupation of Germany gave the United States the power to insist on such an arrangement, and Germany had little power to resist it. The variation in the degree of hierarchy across the three cases is consistent with the argument that relative power is all that the United States needed in order to create a hierarchy. But other elements of the process of negotiating sharing agreements and the outcomes are not so consistent. Little of the process-tracing evidence supports the idea that the Americans universally preferred hierarchical arrangements. The United States does not seem to have pressed Britain for a more hierarchical arrangement during the negotiation of the UKUSA agreement. The United States also offered important benefits to both Britain and West Germany in exchange for taking the dominant position in their intelligence-sharing relationships. While the United States clearly did have greater power resources than the three European countries, it negotiated rather than imposed hierarchical sharing on its partners.

3 INTELLIGENCE SHARING FOR COUNTERINSURGENCY

VIETNAM AND COLOMBIA

This chapter analyzes how and why governments cooperating in fighting an armed insurgency can effectively share intelligence. Countries facing armed opposition on their territory—what I term *host countries*—often obtain military and intelligence assistance from allied states. Since the Second World War, the United States has used substantial diplomatic, military, and intelligence resources to help host countries fight insurgencies. Major American commitments include aid to South Vietnam in the 1960s and 1970s; to Central American countries fighting insurgencies in the 1980s; and to antinarcotics and counterinsurgency efforts in Colombia, Peru, and Bolivia at various times since the 1980s and in Iraq and Afghanistan more recently. Intelligence sharing is very important to counterinsurgency, and organizing intelligence sharing hierarchically can offer host and ally both more and better intelligence by addressing the bargaining and enforcement problems. The existing research on counterinsurgency does not recognize how states have used hierarchy to facilitate their cooperation or does not analyze its costs and benefits.

For analysis, I have selected American cooperation with South Vietnam in the late 1960s and early 1970s and with Colombia since the late 1990s, as they are good cases for evaluating the relational contracting explanation of intelligence sharing. Recall that this theory expects states to propose a hierarchical relationship for sharing intelligence when they each stand to gain from sharing, have strong concerns about their partner's reliability, and conclude that the costs of creating and maintaining the hierarchy are smaller than the joint gains they could expect. The United States' collaboration with South Vietnam and Colombia conforms to this explanation, but it does *not* conform to the explanation of hierarchy that holds that more powerful states always impose this organizational form on subordinate states. The United States' power relative to that of South Vietnam and Colombia did not change substantially during the periods considered here, but its interest in hierarchy did change with its perception of the gains available and the likelihood that its partner would defect.

INTELLIGENCE SHARING AND COUNTERINSURGENCY

Insurgents do not have sufficient military power to defeat their opponents on the battlefield. To compensate, they exploit their ability to launch surprise attacks and to conceal themselves in rough terrain and among the civilian population. Governments can counter the insurgents' use of surprise and concealment effectively only if they have accurate information about their opponents' plans and bases. All the most respected work on counterinsurgency emphasizes the importance of intelligence for this task.[1]

Much of the collection and analysis of intelligence for counterinsurgency is labor intensive. It relies on the authorities' being able to interact regularly with the population and is most successful when the police and military can safely live and work in areas where insurgents are active. Since insurgencies usually hide among civilians and rely on them for support, persuading these noncombatants to give government agencies intelligence on the identity, location, and activities of insurgents is crucial. The authorities rely on interrogations of captured enemy personnel and on captured enemy documents and may also try to cultivate informants within the insurgency. Even though human sources of intelligence are crucial to counterinsurgency operations, more technical approaches to collecting and analyzing intelligence can be useful as well. The authorities may construct databases that allow intelligence analysts and military and police personnel to identify individual insurgents or to track their opponents' political maneuvers and goals, military tactics, weapons, finances, and support from overseas. Aerial reconnaissance and satellite imagery can monitor borders, track insurgents' movements and activities, and prepare detailed maps for military operations. Sensor technology may also help track the movement of insurgents in remote areas. Intercepting telephone, radio, and other forms of communication can provide inside information about the insurgency's organization.

The host country typically has a stronger capability in the collection of human intelligence, as its personnel should be able to speak the languages of the civilian population, be familiar with the terrain, regularly inter-act with civilians, and have a wider array of punishments and rewards with which to control defectors, informants, and agents.[2] In the cases analyzed in this chapter, the United States had a comparative advantage in technical support for intelligence as well as the financial resources to expand the host's intelligence efforts. These advantages thus formed a natural division of labor between the two types of countries, with the host concentrating on collecting human intelligence and the United States financially supporting the host and gathering technical intelligence.[3]

What are the implications of implementing such a division of labor? A technocratic perspective holds that both the host and the ally have a strong interest in defeating the insurgency. Consequently, each should have a similarly strong interest in supplying its partner with relevant in-telligence. Sharing is thus primarily a technical and organizational prob-lem rather than a political problem. After the host and ally agree on the mechanisms to share intelligence efficiently, once such mechanisms are in place the relevant intelligence should flow freely between them. This perspective is often implicit in campaign histories written by military professionals, who, because of their training and background, spend less effort discussing political divisions between allies and more on the tech-nical requirements of their military and intelligence agencies in order to achieve their shared political objectives.[4]

Another explanation centers on how political differences between the host and the ally may actually create incentives to renege on a promise to share intelligence. Although they both want to defeat the insurgency, they may favor different policies for doing so. For example, one may be willing to pay more than the other to achieve victory, or they may face in-ternal difficulties in implementing an agreed-on counterinsurgency policy. These differences can tempt either one to refuse to share intelligence.

Organizational and political barriers in the host country have attracted the most attention. An effective counterinsurgency requires a willingness to expose government forces to attack and to continually defend civilian areas from insurgent activity. The host nation's security forces often lack the proper organization and training required for an effective counterinsurgency; indeed, such weaknesses are an important reason why insurgencies are able to take root in the first place.[5] The military must be willing to seek out and engage the enemy rather than remain in its garrisons or patrol only during daylight hours. Counterinsurgency also requires military leaders to innovate. Because it is difficult to predict the insurgents' location or activities, military leaders must be able and willing to exploit tactical advantages and new intelligence on short notice. But the host nation's military is often not up to these tasks and so may distort or limit shared intelligence to mask its battlefield inadequacies from foreign supporters. Inadequate funding, training, and organization may also lead the hosts' intelligence agencies to do a poor job of collating and analyzing intelligence from multiple sources, which may be considered defection to the extent that the host fails to exploit all its intelligence advantages.

Another organizational weakness is corruption. Corrupt militaries and other government bureaucracies may share intelligence with the enemy or withhold intelligence they obtain from their ally for financial gain. Insurgents also find it easy to insert agents in corrupt bureaucracies. The host country's political leaders themselves may have disagreements or differ from its professional military on how best to defeat the insurgents. They may differ over which or how many resources should be devoted to the counterinsurgency, their resolve in achieving victory, or the desirability of trying to reach a compromise with their armed opponents. Such political divisions can be powerful reasons not to share intelligence with the ally. Political or military leaders favoring compromise, for example, may share intelligence with the insurgents in an attempt to broker a peace deal, or they may withhold relevant intelligence on the insurgency from the ally. Hard-liners may distort their intelligence in order to manipulate the ally's conclusions about the performance of government forces or the capacity of the insurgency to fight. Political leaders worried about threats to their rule from the military or competitors within the government often limit the flow of intelligence so as to maintain their authority. In turn, this may create competing internal intelligence agencies that may fail to share information with one another or the ally.

Allied countries also may have reasons to renege. The ally may not be as strongly resolved to defeat the insurgents as is the host government, whose position in power is directly threatened by insurgency. The ally may have regional interests that conflict with its willingness to prosecute the counterinsurgency vigorously. The ally may also prefer strategies and tactics that differ from those favored by the host nation. The host government, for example, may adopt a policy of brutalizing the civilian population into subservience, and the ally may object to this approach as immoral or an ineffective way to conduct the counterinsurgency. The ally may advocate internal reforms that threaten the host government's political position, such as reducing corruption or training its military forces or integrating rather than compartmentalizing its security agencies, all of which could threaten the host government's hold on power. These conflicts of interest with the host may lead the ally to restrict intelligence sharing for fear that it will be leaked to the insurgents by corrupt host government officials, obtained by the insurgency's agents within the security services, or used to support unwanted military operations. Finally, the ally may withhold relevant intelligence from the host as way to extract greater concessions regarding military strategy and tactics or government reform.

These differences between host and ally have important implications for their willingness to share information about the insurgents. Political conflicts can create incentives for one or both parties to renege on the presumption that they will share all relevant intelligence. Some argue that the only effective solution to such conflicts is to eschew sharing. Daniel Byman, for example, advises that

> to help overcome these problems [of defection], the United States should try to increase its intelligence on allied security forces so that it can better understand the true nature of their activities. To reduce its vulnerability to manipulation, the United States should also try to diversify its intelligence sources to ensure that it does not rely exclusively on the local ally for information.[6]

In other words, concerns about defection may lead the host or ally or both to limit the intelligence that they share, conduct counterintelligence operations on each other, or replace intelligence that their partner could or did supply with intelligence generated by their own agencies.

Neither of these perspectives considers another way in which partners could structure their intelligence sharing: hierarchy. The technocratic understanding posits that the host and ally agree on major objectives and strategies, sees no strong political barriers to full sharing and expects that the participating countries can easily work out mutually acceptable mechanisms, and finds no political reason why one country should take the lead in organizing or overseeing these activities. The second, more political explanation concludes that the optimal solution to the possibility of defection is to limit sharing. But as discussed in chapter 1, hierarchy is an additional organizational form that can mitigate allies' concerns about defection. It can serve the interests of all parties by placing one in a dominant position to manage and oversee the collection, analysis, and sharing of intelligence. As I demonstrate next, states cooperating in counterinsurgency commonly create hierarchical forms. Nonetheless, the focus of the prevailing political approach to how different interests drive allies to seek independent intelligence capabilities blinds analysis to the possibility that hierarchy can be voluntary.

The remainder of this chapter evaluates this argument using case studies of intelligence sharing between the United States and South Vietnam during the late 1960s and with Colombia in the 1990s. The South Vietnam case is useful for evaluating the argument regarding hierarchy, for three reasons. First, the United States changed its policy in 1967 to place greater emphasis on effective intelligence sharing with the South Vietnamese government. U.S. strategy previously relied most heavily on air strikes and offensive "search and destroy" missions to locate and engage insurgent forces. This strategy attached little importance to South Vietnamese military action and intelligence. The fact that the United States did not share intelligence with South Vietnam gave it little incentive to address the consequences of its partner's defection. But by 1967, political and military setbacks had forced the United States to adopt a counterinsurgency doctrine, termed at the time *pacification*, that centered on creating a secure environment for South Vietnamese citizens so they would not support the insurgents. Successful implementation of this strategy required close cooperation with the South Vietnamese government's intelligence and security agencies, which were assigned responsibility for most human intelligence and for local security. This meant that intelligence collaboration with South Vietnam became much more valuable to the United States and that concerns about South Vietnamese defection became a more important influence on American policy. As discussed in chapter 1, this combination of potentially large mutual gains and serious concerns about defection is conductive to the formation of a hierarchical relationship. The fact that after 1967 the United States created important elements of hierarchy in its intelligence-sharing relationship with South Vietnam demonstrates that the explanation of intelligence sharing based on relational contracting advanced here can help us to better understand the conditions facilitating intelligence sharing.

Second, many of the other variables that might influence the extent of U.S.–South Vietnamese cooperation, including their relative power, their interests in the outcome of the conflict, and how each party was motivated to defect, did not change along with the shift in strategy toward pacification. The fact that these other potential influences remain constant across these two cases shows that the relationship of mutual gains, defection, and hierarchy is causal and not spurious.

The third reason I chose South Vietnam is the wealth of declassified documents and secondary accounts available for this case. Owing to its importance to the subsequent evolution of American foreign policy, the South Vietnam experience is often used to illustrate the nature of insurgency and counterinsurgency. Yet none of these accounts has drawn attention to the role of hierarchy in structuring the relationship. Relational contracting provides a theoretically grounded explanation why states would structure their relationship as a hierarchy and thereby provides a richer and more accurate understanding of the dynamics of this case.

Next, to control for a competing explanation of hierarchy, I analyze the United States' and Colombia's more recent sharing of intelligence. One might argue that dominant powers always insist on creating a hierarchical relationship with their subordinates. The South Vietnam case does not allow us to distinguish the role of power asymmetries from other motives for hierarchy. The United States was able to exercise a great deal of influence over its subordinate, as it was directly involved in the conflict, with substantial military forces and enormous amounts of military and economic assistance that propped up the South Vietnamese regime. American involvement in Colombia, though substantial, is considerably smaller. The United States has committed many fewer of its military and intelligence personnel and financial and technical resources to the conflict. The survival of the Colombian government does not depend on American support to the same extent as did the South Vietnamese government, so the power imbalance between the dominant and subordinate states is much smaller. The United States and Colombia created a hierarchical relationship similar in many ways to that formed with South Vietnam, even though the United States' ability to *demand* this outcome was much weaker, because of factors other than the differences in their power resources.

SOUTH VIETNAM

Benefits of Sharing Intelligence

Sharing intelligence was crucial to the pacification strategy that the United States adopted in 1967. Both South Vietnam and the United States could contribute valuable intelligence that the other found too expensive and difficult to collect. Key to successful pacification was collecting intelligence that allowed the authorities to identify members of what was known in official circles as the "Viet Cong infrastructure" (VCI). The VCI consisted of the enemy political leaders and guerrilla forces that used the cover of the South Vietnamese population to hide their identity, location, and activities while planning and carrying out political and military activities designed to undermine the South Vietnamese government. It also included agents and sympathizers in the police, military, and government, forcing the government to monitor the activities of its own personnel. Good intelligence, therefore, allowed the United States and South Vietnam to bring their superior military and organizational resources directly to bear against the forces seeking to undermine the South Vietnam government.

South Vietnam contributed staff with skills useful for collecting and analyzing intelligence at the local level, existing intelligence networks, and programs to facilitate the defection and resettlement of enemy personnel. The joint effort against the Viet Cong infrastructure was able to draw on South Vietnamese military officers, intelligence personnel, police officers, and other civil servants to collect intelligence. As natives of the country, many of these government officials had a detailed knowledge of local languages and cultural practices, social and family ties, and terrain, all of which were very useful for collecting and analyzing intelligence. In addition, there were also far more such South Vietnamese than their American counterparts. South Vietnamese government agencies—including the army, special police, and central intelligence organization—had been in conflict with the Viet Cong for many years and brought their existing networks of agents to the pacification strategy.

The South Vietnamese government ran a defector program known as Chieu hoi (Open Arms) to encourage Viet Cong cadres to abandon the struggle against the government and to give it intelligence, and it used identification card schemes to track the movement of individuals in the country.[7] The United States would have been unable to collect much intelligence useful to the pacification campaign without the active collaboration of the South Vietnamese government.

The United States had a comparative advantage in skills, money, and technology. The American intelligence community contained many experienced intelligence analysts familiar with techniques for collecting, organizing, and analyzing large amounts of information. Its capability to organize a large-scale intelligence effort was very useful for the pacification campaign, which relied on the authorities' being able to create reliable identification documents, build files on individual members of the Viet Cong infrastructure, and track their successes and failures in winning over the countryside. The United States also had sufficient financial resources to develop an effective intelligence infrastructure for the war, including the deployment of many civilian and military intelligence personnel to South Vietnam and funding to train South Vietnamese intelligence officers in the military and police. The United States also had technological assets valuable to the pacification campaign: aerial reconnaissance of the theater to detect the movement of supplies and soldiers to the forces fighting the South Vietnamese government, intercepts of enemy radio communications, and information technology to keep track of the VCI's organization and personnel.[8]

Incentives to Defect

The United States had serious concerns about the South Vietnamese reneging on their joint intelligence effort, especially because its pacification strategy relied heavily on intelligence best collected by South Vietnam. Earlier experience provided many well-documented concerns about South Vietnam's reliability when sharing intelligence. These concerns were the political orientation of South Vietnamese leaders, the effectiveness of the South Vietnamese military, corruption, and the organization of the South Vietnamese intelligence effort.

The South Vietnamese government was organizationally and politically weak, was subject to frequent coups or attempted coups, and had difficulty translating new policies—such as pacification—into concrete action. These shortcomings made it difficult for Americans to trust that some of their South Vietnamese counterparts would treat shared intelligence securely and would themselves pass along only reliable intelligence. The division of the army into political cliques and the almost constant plotting of coups distracted political and military leaders from the struggle with the Communists. On taking office, each new South Vietnamese government would purge military officers and civil servants to ensure that its subordinates were loyal, which made it difficult to ensure continuity in the implementation of public policy. South Vietnamese officials, including the officer corps, had different opinions about how the war should be prosecuted, with many preferring the pursuit of negotiations with the enemy, contrary to the policy of the United States in the mid- and late 1960s. Consequently, some Americans worried that such officers might compromise the security of shared intelligence with the aim of undermining the official strategy that eschewed negotiations.[9]

Corruption was widespread among South Vietnamese officials and allowed the enemy to recruit agents from within the South Vietnamese government who could pass along shared intelligence provided by the United States or prevent the collection of useful intelligence. The South Vietnamese police, for example, compromised security by accepting bribes for releasing captured Viet Cong suspects, for allowing Viet Cong personnel and supplies to pass at checkpoints, and for issuing identification documents. Although the South Vietnamese government had a program that rewarded defectors and individuals who identified Viet Cong weapons caches, officials began organizing phony defectors for financial gain not long after it was introduced.[10] A CIA report in 1970 estimated that there were at least thirty thousand enemy agents in the South Vietnamese government.[11]

American political and military leaders had a low opinion of the South Vietnamese military. The South Vietnamese army had a high rate of desertion and draft evasion, was reluctant to put units into battle and preferred to keep them near their garrisons, often refused to patrol at night, and was led by a politicized and corrupt officer corps. In 1966, for example, the United States privately estimated that fully a third of the South Vietnamese army was unsatisfactory or of marginal effectiveness, calling into question its ability to undertake the roles assigned to it by the pacification strategy. It also undermined American trust in the intelligence provided by the South Vietnamese, who in order to mask their own failures, might share only intelligence that overestimated the threat they faced.[12]

Finally, organizational and political factors created incentives for South Vietnamese intelligence organizations to hoard information rather than to share it with one another and the United States. Military commanders often refused to share information with one another, preferring to bring valuable intelligence directly to the president. These commanders worried, too, that other South Vietnamese and American agencies might use shared intelligence to learn the identity of, and recruit or inadvertently reveal the identities of, their agents providing intelligence on the VCI. Organizational mechanisms for sharing intelligence among the South Vietnamese military, police, and intelligence agencies were poorly developed, and routines for sharing between American and South Vietnamese agencies were even more problematic. One senior South Vietnamese military officer later wrote that "although normal exchange [between the United States and South Vietnam] of current information occurred as a matter of standard operating procedure at all combined intelligence agencies, there was definitely a lack of sharing when it came to important information of immediate consequence."[13]

South Vietnam also worried about the United States' willingness to share intelligence. Because American support was crucial to the survival of the South Vietnamese regime, the South Vietnamese were limited in how much they could defy U.S. wishes. South Vietnamese attempts to block the shift to pacification, such as not sharing enough intelligence to make this policy effective, might have frustrated the United States enough to reduce its commitment to the regime. The South Vietnamese leadership also worried that the United States might intervene in its domestic politics to make sure that the government was committed to its preferred strategy, as it had in 1961 when it encouraged the coup against President Ngo Dinh Diem. The fact that the United States had large and independently commanded military forces in South Vietnam, as well as naval aircraft and air force bombers based outside the country, enabled it to prosecute the war as it wanted, despite the wishes of the South Vietnamese government.[14] These factors led South Vietnamese President Nguyen Van Thieu to support the internal reforms needed for the pacification policy. He realized that the United States was set on the idea of pacification and worried that opposing it might alienate his patron. He also realized that achieving pacification would recommit the

United States to the struggle in South Vietnam and that it would continue to provide material support to the regime. Thieu was not forced by
the United States to take these actions; instead, he shared many of his
American advisers' concerns. Like them, he recognized that the policy
of search and destroy was not effective, especially after the surprise Tet
offensive of 1968, which relied heavily on the VCI operating in South
Vietnam. Thus while the decision to shift to pacification and to increase
dramatically the sharing of intelligence was made by the Americans, it
did have the support of at least the leadership of South Vietnam, which
recognized that subordinating itself to American leadership was necessary
to ensure that the United States remained committed to the struggle.[15]

Search and Destroy: Intelligence-Sharing Outcomes

Before about mid-1967, the American civilian and military leadership
viewed the struggle in South Vietnam as a conventional military conflict.
They believed that the United States and South Vietnamese could prevail by destroying enemy troops and equipment and thus defeating enemy
on the battlefield. The U.S. military's strengths were using its high-tech
weapons, better-trained soldiers, and mobility to bring the fight to the
enemy through bombings and search and destroy missions. Efforts at pacification were secondary. The United States expected South Vietnamese
forces to hold the territory that they cleared of enemy forces but not to
be substantially involved in combat operations. The political and organizational weaknesses of the South Vietnamese forces were partly why the
United States adopted this approach, to replace poorly performing local
forces with American bombers and ground troops. Clearly, the United
States attached little importance to the South Vietnamese military's contribution to the conflict, and sharing intelligence was not a priority. The
United States therefore did not worry much about the South Vietnamese
reneging on intelligence-sharing arrangements and did not attempt to
create a more hierarchical relationship between the two countries' military and intelligence efforts.

Shortly before U.S. ground forces began arriving in large numbers in
1965, American officials discussed creating a combined United States–
South Vietnamese military command. They saw as their model the joint
command used in the Korean War, which gave the United States the

power to direct the efforts of both countries and to fire poorly performing Korean commanders. Secretary of Defense Robert McNamara thought that a joint command would allow the United States to better supervise South Vietnam's actions and inactions, including those related to intelligence sharing. But the American commander in Vietnam, General William Westmoreland, opposed the suggestion of a combined command that would place him at the head of both countries' forces. He thought that a combined command would be viewed as an infringement on South Vietnam's sovereignty and would therefore be opposed by some political forces in the country. Westmoreland also drew attention to the difficulties of organizing staffs from different countries. But an important reason for his position, which he did not emphasize so as not to embarrass the South Vietnamese, was the security of shared intelligence. Westmoreland told his commanders in 1965 that "if the Vietnamese are brought into U.S. operations far in advance, compromise is probable," and a memo written by his command in Vietnam concluded that "no plan can be considered secure" if it is shared with the South Vietnamese. The fact that the United States planned and carried out major military operations during this period largely independently of its South Vietnamese counterparts reduced the possible benefits of making many South Vietnamese privy to their plans. The American and South Vietnamese armies agreed instead to appoint "special representatives" to each other's staffs, but these representatives would have little influence or do much to promote the coordination of military and intelligence activities.[16]

The American and South Vietnamese militaries did combine their intelligence centers to interrogate prisoners, study captured documents and equipment, and analyze intelligence, and they were designed to draw on American strengths in technical collection and analysis and Vietnamese knowledge of local culture. But these combined centers never worked well. They did not draw up clear rules for sharing: The United States often refused to share the intelligence it collected through technical means, and the South Vietnamese bypassed established channels for sharing in order to communicate intelligence directly to politicians. Moreover, the CIA regularly recruited agents in the South Vietnamese army and police. Since the South Vietnamese security agencies did not share intelligence with the United States, these agents gave the Americans some insight into the intelligence they had collected.[17]

Pacification: Intelligence-Sharing Outcomes

The United States' pacification strategy was based on classic counterinsurgency doctrine. Although search and destroy presumed that American
forces could locate the enemy, the Viet Cong relied on indirect methods
to achieve their aims. Rather than confront government and American
military forces, they used guerrilla warfare, terrorism, and assassination to
exhaust and frighten their opponents. Pacification was intended to collect intelligence that would allow the authorities to oppose these tactics
by first identifying and then detaining, turning, or killing members of the
VCI. American authorities recognized that for it to succeed, this strategy
needed close intelligence cooperation between the United States and
South Vietnam.[18]

Both sides, but especially the United States, worried that defection
by the other would undermine such cooperation, so the solution was to
make their intelligence-sharing relationship more hierarchical. Hierarchy facilitated the mutually beneficial exchange of intelligence on the
VCI by addressing each state's concern about the defection of the other.
Hierarchy allowed the United States to more closely monitor and direct
South Vietnam's intelligence activities. It also meant that the United
States could try to improve the intelligence capabilities and security of
the South Vietnamese government's agencies and military forces. At the
same time, the pacification strategy reassured the South Vietnamese that
the United States remained committed to aiding its ally in its political
and military struggle.

From the U.S. perspective, an important objective of the shift to pacification was strengthening South Vietnamese government's legitimacy
among the population and its capacity to address its internal security
problems. But this effort risked creating the impression among the South
Vietnamese leadership that the United States' true objective was to wind
down its commitment to a conflict that was becoming very unpopular.
The manner in which the United States developed a more hierarchical
relationship with South Vietnam addressed this concern. The United
States publicly recommitted itself to continuing to work with the South
Vietnamese. This meant that the United States' reputation would suffer
if it were seen to abruptly abandon its ally. Even after President Richard M. Nixon announced in 1969 a policy of "Vietnamization" aimed at

transferring greater responsibilities to the regime in Saigon, the United States maintained large numbers of military forces in the country and continued to give the regime financial and military assistance. American authorities also made it clear that this new strategy could not work without the active collaboration of the South Vietnamese. This meant that the United States was more reliant on its ally and thus more vulnerable to any defection. This position further reassured the South Vietnamese that the shift to pacification was not simply a prelude to an American withdrawal in the near future and that the United States remained engaged in the conflict.

Although they do not use the term hierarchy, the internal studies and discussions that led to the adoption of the pacification strategy clearly recognized the need for it, arguing that successful pacification would require the United States to exert more leverage to induce South Vietnamese compliance.[19] As one internal analysis explained,

> Much more can be accomplished by integration, unified management and joint coordination of the various programs . . . [and] can generate substantial influence and pressure on the [South Vietnamese government] at all levels to bring about an effective and coordinated operation against the VC infrastructure. For unified direction and for high-impact management of the various programs, reporting and information systems must be centrally designed, administered and controlled, and information specifications and criteria must be established centrally.[20]

The United States took four steps after 1967 to give it more leverage over the South Vietnamese government to improve its intelligence sharing in support of pacification. First, it increased the number of and importance of U.S. military and intelligence advisers.[21] It also began permitting its advisers to accompany South Vietnamese forces on raids and other military actions. The declared objective was to improve the performance of the South Vietnamese military. But these advisers also monitored its South Vietnamese ally's actions on the ground. They were part of the U.S., not the South Vietnamese, chain of command and reported to their superiors about the performance of the units to which they were attached. This meant that the U.S. leadership no longer had to rely on South Vietnamese reports on the tactics used by its military units.

Second, the United States devoted time and resources to reorganizing the South Vietnamese government to carry out the pacification strategy more effectively and to deal with corruption. American officials also encouraged the South Vietnamese to share intelligence among themselves, including urging the South Vietnamese government to establish intelligence coordination centers in each province and district to bring together local officials responsible for administration, police, and civilian and military intelligence and to assemble dossiers on suspected members of the VCI.[22] The United States persuaded the South Vietnamese to raise the status of their police forces which, given their frequent interactions with civilians and role in protecting the public, were a crucial source of intelligence. The American civilian agency in charge of pacification convinced the South Vietnamese government to allow its national police to oversee its own training program and to select its personnel independently of the military, as well as to provide more resources to the special police, the branch most closely involved in pacification. Pressure from American civilian advisers also led to the creation of a ministerial-level pacification council that brought together senior government ministers to coordinate their actions and plans and to encourage the sharing of intelligence among South Vietnamese agencies. American officials also created the Hamlet Evaluation System (HES) to measure the progress of pacification at the village level. The United States insisted on directly developing and maintaining the HES so that it would have a reliable measure of the progress of pacification in the countryside and could prevent South Vietnam from tampering with its structure or data.[23]

Third, the United States and South Vietnam established the jointly operated Phoenix program, which was designed to use intelligence, police work, and military raids to find, turn, imprison, interrogate, or kill members of the VCI. Earlier South Vietnamese efforts in this area had not worked well. The United States believed that captured members of the VCI could buy their freedom from corrupt officials; that the South Vietnamese focused too much effort on rounding up lower-echelon members of the VCI, who could be easily replaced, rather than the leaders; and that they relied too heavily on paid informants for information and used torture and imprisonment indiscriminately, which produced little useful intelligence on the VCI and alienated the South Vietnamese population. The United States instituted procedures to make Phoenix more effective, including creating common rules to determine which individuals actually were members of the VCI, improving the system for maintaining intelligence files on suspected members of the VCI, and favoring payments to informants who provided reliable information about VCI leaders rather than foot soldiers. The United States also tried to change how the South Vietnamese treated suspects it had detained, although there is considerable debate about how successful it was. The United States ordered the South Vietnamese to concentrate on capturing rather than killing members of the VCI so that they could be interrogated for intelligence. It also tried to improve haphazard interrogation techniques and many South Vietnamese military and intelligence personnel's counterproductive use of violence against detainees. In turn, this meant improving the security of detention centers, training South Vietnamese interrogators, directly supervising these interrogators' activities, and having American intelligence officers interrogate detainees directly or through interpreters.[24]

Both direct and indirect evidence indicates that hierarchy led to greater intelligence sharing between the United States and South Vietnam after the pacification strategy was adopted in 1967. American officials believed that the strategy was effective; while problems remained, especially corruption, their overall assessment was that pacification made the South Vietnamese more effective.[25] Rural security improved: between 1968 and 1970, the percentage of rural residents living in villages judged to be relatively secure rose by 20 percent. The Phoenix program captured or killed more than eighty thousand suspected members of the VCI, and in accordance with American policy, many more were captured, and thus offered more possible intelligence value, than were killed outright. For its part, South Vietnam shifted more of its counterinsurgency to the leaders of the VCI.

Pacification also led to a change in the enemy's strategy. Until about 1970, the North Vietnamese employed a strategy of insurgency that relied very heavily on the VCI. After 1970, though, they turned to a more conventional military strategy of confronting South Vietnamese and American units directly on the battlefield. This change in strategy was driven in large part by the success of pacification in curtailing the VCI's activities.[26] Pacification also succeeded in shifting more of the combat burden from American military units that attacked enemy forces to South Vietnamese forces supported by American advisers and air power.[27]

The Marines in Vietnam

After 1966, U.S. Marines were assigned to defend areas of northern South Vietnam, and they adopted a counterinsurgency strategy in some areas based on many of the pacification policy's principles, well before and independently of this strategy was adopted by all American civilian agencies and ground forces operating in South Vietnam. The marines' experience provides additional evidence that can be used to evaluate the expectation of relational contracting that parties develop hierarchical intelligence-sharing arrangements when the possible mutual gains are high but the concerns about defection are substantial.[28]

The marines' Combined Action Program (CAP) assigned a marine rifle squad and a platoon of indigenous militia forces to protect a single village. These combined units trained, patrolled, defended, and lived together in the village with the objective of eliminating local VCI forces, providing security to the population, and gathering intelligence from the residents. The goal of providing security was crucial to gathering intelligence, as it convinced the residents that they would be protected from reprisals by the VCI and no longer would have to provide intelligence on the authorities' actions to the VCI.

By cooperating, the marines and South Vietnamese militias could help each other by sharing intelligence. The militias could translate for the marines questioning villagers or interrogating suspected members of the VCI (very few marines spoke Vietnamese or received any language training).[29] The South Vietnamese also were better at eliciting intelligence from cooperative villagers and could help the marines put this information in the proper context by, for example, explaining which locals were the most prominent or most likely to have useful information. Members of the militia had better knowledge of the local terrain, which was useful for guiding long-range patrols of marines searching for information about VCI hideouts and weapons caches in remote areas. In return, the marines gave the militias much greater security. South Vietnamese militias were poorly equipped and could not expect quick reinforcement when threatened by enemy forces. The permanent presence of a marine platoon armed with modern weapons and with the ability to call in helicopter reinforcements and air strikes therefore greatly strengthened the militia's morale and helped them fend off enemy incursions.

Both sides worried that the other might renege on this arrangement. Since the CAPs were implemented at the local level, the marines were not concerned with issues such as the poor organization of the South Vietnamese military and intelligence services or the influence of political instability in the country on intelligence sharing. But they did worry about the reliability of local militia members and their units. The marines' security from attack depended in part on the reliability of their militia counterparts, who might betray them if they faced the threat of punishment or the promise of rewards from the VCI. The marines also were concerned that the militia forces might not collect intelligence aggressively or would distort it in order to convince the Americans that the threat from the VCI was greater or smaller than it actually was. The South Vietnamese forces' main concern was the marines' commitment to stay in the villages over the long term. As discussed earlier, the U.S. Army's focus on search and destroy led it to clear the enemy's villages and surrounding countryside and then to leave security to the militia. But this placed the militia in the dangerous situation of having to defend often uncooperative villagers against enemy forces that might outnumber them. Therefore, the militia had little incentive to cooperate actively with the army, since doing so might only lead to reprisals once the army had moved on from the village.

Hierarchy was a good way of addressing these concerns. Basing platoons of American marines in South Vietnamese villages was an inefficient way to implement the pacification strategy. Even without concerns about defection, both the South Vietnamese and the Americans would have been more successful if the marines persuaded the local militias to guard the villages, by giving them training, financing, weapons, and occasional reinforcements. The local militias better understood their enemy, could collect intelligence more easily, and were less expensive to fund and more numerous than the marines.

Although the decision was not described in these terms, the purpose of basing marines in the villages was to create a hierarchical relationship with the South Vietnamese forces to ensure that they did not renege on providing security and sharing intelligence. Inserting marines on long-term assignments allowed them to direct the intelligence efforts of the South Vietnamese militias. The long-term assignment of marines made them more effective, as they were able to learn something about how "their" village functioned. In some cases, it also permitted the marines to develop trusting relationships with their militia counterparts and with local villagers, a point emphasized in many of the studies of the CAPs' experiences in individual villages.[30] This trust facilitated intelligence sharing between the Vietnamese and the Americans, based on their experiences of successfully using an initially hierarchical relationship to overcome concerns about defection.

COLOMBIA

The United States' counternarcotics strategy emphasizes reducing the supply and production of illegal drugs. As part of its effort to control supply, the United States has strengthened its domestic enforcement of drug laws and hardened its borders with Mexico and the Caribbean. It also has tried to reduce the production of cocaine in Latin America before it can be sent to the United States. Much of this effort has focused on Colombia, where drug cartels and local insurgencies have been the largest producers and exporters of cocaine to the United States since the early 1990s.[31]

Beginning in the late 1980s, the illegal cultivation of coca expanded rapidly in Colombia. Criminal organizations, the "drug cartels," manufactured cocaine from this coca and sent it to the United States. The Colombian government also faced a double threat from two military insurgencies, the Fuerzas armadas revolucionarias de Colombia (FARC) and the Ejército de liberación nacional (ELN). In the 1990s, both these groups became closely tied to the drug trade. Their participation in and protection of the drug trade gave them a new source of revenue with which to maintain their military and political activities, and during the next decade they increased their direct involvement in the cultivation of coca and the production of cocaine. The strengthening of their ability to challenge the state's authority prompted some landowners to encourage the development of paramilitary forces that would protect them from insurgents and criminal groups seeking protection money. These paramilitaries then evolved into a more formal group, the Autodefensas unidas de Colombia (AUC). By the end of the decade, however, the AUC was using many of their opponents' tactics, such as demanding protection money and profiting from the drug trade. All three groups were large— collectively having more combatants than the Colombian army—and were well enough funded to mount substantial military efforts in some regions of the country using sophisticated military equipment.[32]

The closer ties between the insurgent groups and the drug traffickers led the United States to devote more attention to Colombia beginning in the mid-1990s. The initial response was "Plan Colombia," passed in 2000, which was supposed to support the Colombian government's efforts against those challenging its authority. Most of the $4.5 billion that the United States gave to Colombia between 2000 and 2005 was used to train Colombian military units and police forces. Although Plan Colombia restricted American assistance to Colombian counternarcotics efforts and prohibited its use in counterinsurgency operations, President George W. Bush's administration dropped this distinction between counternarcotics and counterinsurgency in early 2002, thereby allowing American aid to be used in both types of conflicts.[33]

One reason for this change was the belief that as the ties among traffickers, growers, and insurgents grew closer, it would be impractical and ineffective to target only one sort of enemy. Another was the renewed desire of the Colombian government to prevail in the conflict. In 2000, the Colombian president, Andrés Pastrana, agreed to negotiate with the FARC and, as a gesture of goodwill, withdrew government forces from a section of southern Colombia where the FARC was active. But he abandoned these negotiations in 2002 after concluding that the FARC was unwilling to agree to the concessions that the government demanded. Pastrana was succeeded as president by Álvaro Uribe, who was elected on a promise to step up the government's counterinsurgency and counternarcotics efforts.[34]

An important difference between the South Vietnamese case and the Colombian case is the scale of the U.S. effort. The United States spent tens of billions of dollars and deployed hundreds of thousands of military personnel to fight in South Vietnam. It gave Colombia several billion dollars and sent hundreds, not hundreds of thousands, of civilian and military officials to the country and prohibited its military personnel from engaging in combat operations. This meant that the United States had far less leverage over the Colombian governments than it had had over the South Vietnamese governments. Consequently, the United States had less power to dictate to the Colombians how they should organize their intelligence activities or to insist on a hierarchical arrangement for the two countries to share intelligence. Nonetheless, evidence that

Colombia and the United States did in fact form a hierarchical relationship for intelligence sharing supports the proposition that hierarchy is not simply forced on the weaker partner by the stronger but offers substantial benefits to both compared with other arrangements.

Benefits of Sharing Intelligence

Sharing intelligence is an important way in which the United States and Colombia can combat the activities of the insurgents and the drug traffickers. The criminal organizations and insurgents that run the drug trade in Colombia conceal their activities from the authorities, who seek intelligence on where the crops are grown and processed, on the routes and techniques used to export narcotics, and on the organizations' membership, sources of finance, and interactions with others, such as arms suppliers or corrupt government officials. Insurgents and traffickers both use sophisticated communication technologies and exploit Colombia's rough terrain in order to conceal their activities.[35] Collaboration between the United States and Colombia thus allows them to gather more and better intelligence than each could collect individually. Like the South Vietnamese, the Colombians can provide personnel with the language skills and local knowledge useful to collecting and analyzing intelligence, as well as police and military units that can act on such intelligence by arresting suspects and questioning witnesses and informants. The Colombian authorities benefit from the Americans' contributions of technology, money, and skills. The United States provides aerial monitoring of remote areas of the Colombian countryside used for cultivating and processing cocaine, as well as technology for intercepting electronic communications among traffickers. It funds the Colombian military, police, and intelligence agencies to allow them to expand their counternarcotics efforts, and helps finance economic regeneration in those parts of the country that rely heavily on coca cultivation. It also has the money and expertise to train Colombian authorities in techniques useful for combating counternarcotics and counterinsurgency efforts.

Incentives to Defect

The United States worries that Colombia could betray it in at least three ways. The Colombian government might negotiate agreements with the drug traffickers and the insurgents that would allow them to continue exporting cocaine to the United States. Such agreements would reduce the government's interest in sharing intelligence with the United States or acting aggressively on shared intelligence. Indeed, the Colombian government conducted such negotiations in the past. All the Colombian presidents elected since the late 1970s came to office promising to crack down on the insurgents and traffickers but later negotiated or offered them amnesties. In addition, the Colombian governments in the late 1980s and early 1990s essentially agreed to overlook the criminal activities of some drug cartels if they did not engage in widespread political violence and softened the punishments of others by, for example, not extraditing them to the United States.[36] President Pastrana negotiated with the FARC and ELN in the late 1990s, allowing them to control sections of Colombian territory unmolested by the army and not insisting on their disarming before starting talks. Although the United States initially supported these negotiations with the insurgents, by 2001 it was concerned that their growing ties to the drug traffickers might induce the government to make concessions that would undermine its ability to reduce the flow of cocaine to the United States.[37]

The United States also had concerns about human rights abuses committed by Colombian forces and the paramilitaries. The principal concern here was that a lack of respect for human rights would reduce support within the United States for cooperation on security and intelligence matters with the Colombian authorities. Reports of such abuses were widespread.[38] Consequently, the U.S. Congress prohibited using American funds to support Colombian military units accused of human rights violations, but the State Department had difficulty identifying effective units without such problems.[39] The paramilitary forces grouped under the AUC also presented a human rights problem, since they were known by American authorities to commit violations and to have links to the Colombian military.[40]

Corruption was the third way in which Colombia could undermine intelligence sharing. Drug traffickers used their wealth to corrupt politicians and public officials in the police, military, judiciary, and intelligence agencies. The United States worried that these individuals might not act on intelligence shared by the United States or would betray the source of the intelligence to the drug traffickers. Related to corruption was the low level of the Colombian security agencies' professionalism and dedication to counternarcotics and counterinsurgency. In particular, the Colombian army was criticized for being poorly trained and having too few soldiers assigned to combat units.[41]

Colombian authorities likewise were concerned that the United States would renege, although these concerns were mitigated by the strong preference of the United States to address the issue of illegal drugs by reducing the supply from overseas. The Colombian authorities worried that the United States would press them to confront its opponents more aggressively, and thus expose them to more political and military danger, but would fail to support their effort. Particularly important here was tying American aid to Colombia's human rights performance and the process of "certifying" Colombia's commitment to end drug trafficking. Failing either of these tests could result in a reduction of American assistance. In fact, the United States had "decertified" Colombia's counternarcotics efforts for three years in the 1990s, although it did not greatly reduce the amount of aid provided during this period.[42] Another Colombian concern was that the United States would begin to take unilateral action against the traffickers, such as by restricting travel and trade between Colombia and the United States or even by launching military attacks against their facilities in Colombia. Steps like these might allow the United States to interdict the flow of cocaine but would have a harmful effect on Colombia's economy and might lead the public to punish the government for its earlier cooperation with the United States.

Outcomes

The United States needed Colombia's active cooperation to achieve its counternarcotics and counterinsurgency objectives. The terms of its assistance prohibited United States personnel from using force in the country and limited the number of American advisers and trainers in the country to well under a thousand. But the United States worried that it could not trust some Colombian politicians, civil servants, and military personnel to live up to their promises to provide such cooperation. As in the case of South Vietnam, the solution was to introduce elements of hierarchy into the intelligence relationship that would allow the United States to monitor Colombia's compliance and give it powerful levers to punish any noncompliance that it detected.

Two elements of the cooperation between United States and Colombia during this period—aerial reconnaissance and training—incorporated hierarchy. Aerial reconnaissance was useful for determining where coca was being illegally cultivated, for tracking and intercepting the small aircraft used to transport cocaine, and for locating the insurgents' and traffickers' headquarters. U.S. government agencies had the relevant experience, much of it developed in the military and in civilian agencies monitoring the Caribbean for drug trafficking in the 1980s. The United States also could more easily afford to finance the infrastructure and equipment and personnel needed for a comprehensive aerial reconnaissance program. The form of the assistance offered by the United States not only made aerial reconnaissance more effective but also gave the Americans valuable tools for monitoring the activities of Colombian security agencies. These agencies were the ones that would act on most of the intelligence gained through aerial reconnaissance.

Participating in the detailed mapping of coca cultivation gave the United States raw data from which it could independently chart the success of the coca eradication program and determine whether the Colombian forces were preventing the coca growers from returning to previously cleared areas. Tracking the flights of suspected drug traffickers and the activities of insurgent military units gave the Americans more information to decide whether Colombian forces were following up on this intelligence. The Americans carefully controlled this intelligence as well, usually denying the Colombians access to all the information they gathered and refusing to release real-time reconnaissance intelligence. Controlling what intelligence they shared with the Colombians gave the Americans an important lever over the targets that the ground forces could identify. For example, until at least late 2002, the United States wanted the Colombians to focus more of their efforts against the drug traffickers than against the political insurgencies. It thus refused to share aerial intelligence on the insurgents with the Colombian military units unless they could be directly connected to narcotics trafficking.[43]

Training the Colombian police, military, and judicial agencies was the largest and most important part of the American assistance. As with aerial reconnaissance and technical assistance, the goal here was to make these units more effective. U.S. military units taught their counterparts counterinsurgency warfare skills, how to plan better operations, and how to use the more advanced military technology they provided.[44] Training did not allow the United States to directly monitor the subsequent actions of the Colombian agencies, but it did give the United States the opportunity to restructure the agencies to reduce future defection.[45]

American training went beyond technical assistance, with the goal of reshaping the organization and missions of the Colombian units. The United States spent most of its training funds to create new units of the Colombian army. The units were specifically trained for counterinsurgency operations, which would make them more effective than other Colombian army units. The intention was to make them not only better than but also different from other Colombian army units. These units were made up of professional soldiers, in contrast to most of the military composed of conscripts. Volunteers wanting to pursue a career with the army would take advantage of the opportunities of special training and would internalize the organization's new goals. Individuals selected for these units were vetted to ensure that they had not been involved in past human rights abuses.[46] By 2003 American officials were convinced that this focus on training had reduced some of their concerns about defection, as the Colombian units were more effective, handled intelligence properly, and engaged in few if any serious human rights abuses.[47]

Conclusions

The success of counterinsurgency campaigns depends on the authorities' ability to collect intelligence. When can states cooperating in counterinsurgency share intelligence? How well does the relational contracting theory of sharing explain it in this context? Consider how intelligence sharing between the United States and Vietnam evolved over time. The most important change here was the shift beginning in 1967 by the United States from the policy of search and destroy to the policy of pacification.

Process tracing of the cases indicates that this change in the overall policy altered the Americans' thinking about intelligence sharing in two, related, ways. First, it caused them to attach a higher value to intelligence sharing with South Vietnam. Pacification demanded more and more detailed intelligence on the activities of the VCI in civilian areas, and South Vietnamese agencies were better equipped to collect and to act on this intelligence. Consistent with the first expectation presented in chapter 1, a large increase in mutual gains was necessary in order for the United States to become interested in sharing intelligence. Second, as expected by the third relational contracting expectation, the now greater benefit of intelligence sharing reduced the net costs of creating and maintaining a hierarchical intelligence relationship between the two countries. In other words, it became worthwhile for the United States to actively monitor South Vietnam's intelligence activities, since doing so would contribute to the success of the pacification program.

At the same time, the shift from search and destroy to pacification did not have a noticeable influence on the incentives of either the United States or South Vietnam to renege on cooperation. Relational contracting expects parties to form a hierarchy in situations like this, in which they face the possibility of large benefits from cooperation, a high likelihood of defection, and lower costs of managing a hierarchy. The United States and South Vietnam moved in this direction after 1966, and before this, the marines in northern South Vietnam displayed a similar pattern at the local level. The most important elements of this new relationship were the Americans' monitoring of or more direct control over the activities of the South Vietnamese through the expansion in number of civilian and military advisers; the creation of objective measures of progress, such as the Hamlet Evaluation System, that could not be easily manipulated to deceive the other country; and the Americans' restructuring of South Vietnamese agencies so that they would improve their gathering, securing, and sharing of intelligence.

This comparison of the search and destroy and pacification periods does not offer much support for alternative explanations of intelligence sharing, because other independent variables that might influence the nature and extent of intelligence sharing did not change much between the two episodes. There was not a noticeable increase in the American authorities' trust in their South Vietnamese counterparts' desire to comply with promises to share intelligence. Instead, the Americans were attracted to hierarchy after 1967 precisely because they could not trust South Vietnam not to defect. Although the degree and form of intelligence sharing changed across the cases of search and destroy and pacification, the degree of mistrust between the United States and South Vietnam remained constant.

The outcomes of the two cases also do not accord with the expectations of neoliberal institutionalism. Neoliberal institutionalism would explain the improvement in intelligence sharing between the United States and South Vietnam after 1967 as the product of the development of new institutions that would improve their ability to detect defection or that would raise the costs of defection. This did happen. For example, the Hamlet Evaluation System allowed the United States to monitor more carefully the performance of South Vietnamese security forces, and the United States provided additional training and technology that it could have threatened to withdraw if the South Vietnamese defected. What neoliberal institutionalism has difficulty explaining is the form of these institutions, which violated the theory's assumption that the relations between states are characterized by anarchy. The Hamlet Evaluation System was not a third party independently evaluating compliance with the pacification program but was a tool for the United States to monitor and correct South Vietnam. U.S. training and technology were intended to make South Vietnamese forces more effective at counterinsurgency, certainly, but also allowed the United States to direct its actions. Neoliberal institutionalism does not regard as a possibility this sort of direct control by one state of some of the decisions and actions of its partner.

Particularly important is the fact the relative power of the United States and South Vietnam did not differ much either before or after 1967. Recall that an important alternative explanation for the outcome of hierarchy is such power imbalances, which allow the more powerful state to insist on creating a hierarchy. Even though the United States had a great deal of leverage over South Vietnam during the search and destroy period, it did not insist on a hierarchical arrangement for sharing intelligence. Only when the Americans shifted to a policy of pacification did the South Vietnamese conclude that the benefits of such a hierarchy would outweigh the costs. Furthermore, their desire to introduce elements of hierarchy was not strongly resisted by the South Vietnamese government, which supported the shift to pacification and recognized that hierarchy would reassure the United States of its willingness to support the new policy.

The case of intelligence sharing with Colombia reinforces this point. Here there was also a power imbalance favoring the United States. But the imbalance was smaller than it was in South Vietnam, and these two countries also were able to agree to create a hierarchy to govern their intelligence sharing. This outcome is consistent with the expectations of relational contracting. From the perspective of the United States, the gains from sharing intelligence with Colombia were large; the United States could not effectively combat the drug-trafficking organizations without the active collaboration of Colombia's intelligence and military agencies. The likelihood of defection was clearly high, due to domestic political pressures on Colombian presidents to engage in negotiations and the corruption that pervaded much of the country's public administration. Introducing hierarchy here has allowed the United States to monitor closely the actions and performance of its counterpart. Such mechanisms, including active control over aerial reconnaissance and the development of new Colombian military units through training, have been relatively modest in terms of governance expense, as they can be introduced and managed by a few hundred American personnel on the ground and at a modest financial cost.

4 INTELLIGENCE SHARING IN THE EUROPEAN UNION
INSTITUTIONS ARE NOT ENOUGH

The collection and analysis of intelligence are increasingly important to the European Union, in order to deal with the many security threats it faces, such as terrorism, the failure of state institutions in the developing world, and the proliferation of weapons of mass destruction. One way of obtaining such intelligence is sharing. Since the 1990s the European Union has created or extended three institutions to encourage and facilitate intelligence sharing among its members: the Berne Group, which brings together the security services of all the member states; the European Police Office (Europol), which collects, shares, and disseminates intelligence on threats such as organized crime and terrorism; and the European Union Military Staff, which analyzes intelligence on overseas developments.

The objective of these institutions is to facilitate the sharing of relevant intelligence by replacing the patchwork of ad hoc and bilateral intelligence-sharing arrangements used by the member states since the 1970s. These institutions create technical mechanisms to disseminate intelligence among national authorities, including organizing regular meetings of ministers and officials, creating common intelligence databases, and sharing information on security practices such as counterterrorism. But these institutions do not tackle the problem of defection.

The European Union thus has constructed anarchic intelligence-sharing institutions, including technical mechanisms that facilitate the sharing of intelligence but do not intrude on the member states' autonomy to decide what intelligence to share or not to share.

One way to help avoid defection would be to share authority over intelligence at the level of the European Union. That is, they could agree to add elements of hierarchy to their intelligence sharing by creating an organization to coordinate each country's intelligence effort and to monitor them, thereby ensuring the member states' compliance with promises to share intelligence. Integrating authority has drawbacks, however. Member states that now are reluctant to share fully with another would also be reluctant to cede authority to a European agency. Moves in this direction also would bring to the fore distributional conflicts about how such an agency would be structured and which country or countries would set its priorities and pay for its activities.

The European Union has succeeded in solving similar bargaining and enforcement problems in other issue areas, like the liberalization of intra-European barriers to trade and the creation of a single European currency. But doing so for intelligence sharing is unlikely. The reason is that the European Union does not have a leading or dominant state that would be willing and able to take the lead in negotiating and managing a more centralized intelligence effort. More likely is a continuation of the current pattern of multispeed cooperation on intelligence. Multispeed cooperation refers to subsets of member states making specific intelligence-sharing arrangements outside the European Union's formal structures.

In this chapter, I first discuss how an integrated European economy that includes the free movement of people, goods, and capital, as well as more tentative steps toward a common security and defense policy, has created stronger incentives for the member states to share intelligence. I then explain how concerns about defection by other member states inhibits what could be mutually beneficial sharing and how European institutions might be designed to overcome this problem. Next I describe the member states' fear of defection by their partners and examine the structure of the European Union's three institutions for sharing intelligence: the Berne Group, Europol, and the European Union Military Staff. There is strong, if indirect, evidence that concerns about defection are in fact a barrier to intelligence sharing in the European Union and that none of the existing institutions can overcome such concerns. Finally, I describe two ways in which these institutions could be reformed to make intelligence sharing more effective. The first is to increase their independent powers to supervise and monitor the member states' intelligence collection, analysis, and sharing. The development of a hierarchical European Union intelligence capability is likely to be strongly opposed by the individual national governments, which are concerned about whether they would be adequately rewarded for their cooperation. Instead, I believe that encouraging more secure sharing among smaller groups of member states is a more realistic medium-term response.

INCENTIVES TO SHARE INTELLIGENCE IN THE EUROPEAN UNION

Since the early 1990s, two sets of developments have created stronger incentives for member states to share intelligence. First, the European Union instituted the free movement of people among its member states and a single market for capital, goods and services, and a single currency. These actions have reduced national controls on cross-border activities and created a demand for intelligence about transnational terrorism and other criminal activities.[1] Second, the development of a European Union defense and security policy has led the member states to combine some aspects of their defense policy planning, including intelligence on overseas developments.

The free circulation of goods, capital, and people within the European Union poses four challenges to the member states' internal security. The first is that it allows organized crime groups to increase the scale of their activities overseas without fear of detection at intra-European Union borders. The second threat, which in many cases is closely related to the first, is that it eliminates an opportunity to detect illegal trafficking in drugs, people, or items like counterfeit goods and components of weapons of mass destruction. Third, the introduction of a single currency and the creation of a single financial market make it easier for criminal or terrorist groups to launder money or to move overseas funds gained through illicit activities.[2] The fourth concern relates to terrorism. Free movement makes it easier for terrorists targeting one member state to seek a safe haven in another member state. It also makes it easier for international terrorist groups outside Europe to communicate with one another and organize their activities across the member states.[3]

The second major change with implications for intelligence sharing is the development of common foreign and security policies. The key step for intelligence sharing was the European Security and Defense Policy (ESDP), which was established in November 1998 at the bilateral summit between British Prime Minster Tony Blair and French President Jacques Chirac in Saint-Malo, France. The two leaders issued a joint declaration regarding European defense which stated that "the Union must have the capacity for autonomous action, backed up by credible military forces, the means to use them, and a readiness to do so, in order to respond to international crises." The changes to the European Union's responsibilities they envisioned were substantial, including the development of "appropriate structures and a capacity for analysis of situations, sources of intelligence, and a capability for relevant strategic planning."

INTELLIGENCE SHARING IN THE EUROPEAN UNION

Do the member states of the European Union believe that their partners have incentives to defect from agreements to share intelligence? How, if at all, do European Union institutions facilitate sharing by countering any such incentives to defection? The Berne Group, Europol, and the European Union Military Staff were created to support technical facilities for sharing intelligence, but they cannot stop defection by member states' intelligence agencies. When the member states created these institutions, they were careful not to include any requirements for sharing intelligence. One reason was that the governments worried that their partners might defect in the future, which made them wary about committing themselves to share intelligence freely with all other member states of the Union. This interpretation of why European institutions do not directly address concerns about defection is based on evidence from the actual collaboration of member states' intelligence agencies and public statements by government officials.

Sharing Institutions

The Berne Group, or the Club of Berne, was formed in the 1970s as a forum for the security services of six European Union member states. It now has twenty-seven members, that is, all the European Union member states, with the chair of the group rotating in tandem with that of the Union. The Berne Group serves as the principal point of contact of the heads of the national security services, who meet regularly under its auspices. The group has established working groups on terrorism and organized crime and in 2001 created the Counterterrorist Group (CTG) in which the member states, as well as the United States, offer common threat assessments that are shared among the membership and some Union committees.[4] The Berne Group does not base its activities on a formal charter and operates outside the European Union's institutions. It does not appear to contain a formal commitment, or even an expectation, that the participants will share all their relevant intelligence with the other members.

The European Police Organization, or Europol, was created in 1995 by a convention signed by all member states and began operations in 1999. The predecessor of Europol was the Trevi Group, created by the member states in the 1970s as a part of European Political Cooperation. Trevi was an intergovernmental forum with no role for the commission, or European parliament. Instead, the member states' interior ministries and security services used the Trevi Group to coordinate national counterterrorism efforts that had cross-border implications. Trevi established secure communication links among member states to share intelligence on terrorism and sponsored the exchange of information on training, equipment, and investigative methods. Like the Berne Group, Trevi had no formal requirement that states share relevant intelligence and no permanent secretariat or staff, and it did not analyze intelligence independently.[5]

Europol's priorities are illegal trafficking in drugs, human beings, and vehicles; illegal immigration; terrorism; and forgery, money laundering, and cyber crimes that cross national borders.[6] Its principal objective is to improve the sharing of intelligence on these matters among member states rather than engaging in security, police, or counterterrorism operations directly. It encourages intelligence sharing by obtaining and analyzing intelligence provided by the member states, notifying them when it has "information concerning them and of any connections identified between criminal offences," providing "strategic intelligence" and preparing "general situation reports," and, since April 2002, establishing ad hoc teams of staff from Europol and interested member states to collect shared intelligence on specific terrorist groups.[7] Europol has a staff of about sixty-five analysts as well as an equal number of staff borrowed from national governments.[8]

Each member state is represented at Europol headquarters by a European liaison officer (ELO). Member states are required to supply relevant intelligence to Europol through their ELOs, either on their own initiative or in response to a request from the organization. ELOs also are responsible for filing national requests for information from Europol. The key mechanism for intelligence sharing is the European Computer System (TECS), which contains two types of intelligence. The first is the Europol Information System, which contains information about individuals and groups suspected of having committed, or being likely to commit, a crime falling under Europol's jurisdiction. This information is limited to basic identifying characteristics (such as name, date and place of birth, nationality, and sex) as well as information about crimes committed or likely to be committed, suspected membership in criminal organizations, and relevant convictions.[9] The second type of intelligence is "work files" generated by Europol staff and ELOs dealing with the details of specific offenses, including suspects' contacts, potential witnesses, and other relevant information.

Intelligence sharing to support the European Security and Defense Policy centers on the European Union Military Staff, which supports the Military Committee and the Political and Security Committee. The Military Staff has an Intelligence Division of about thirty people responsible for early warning, assessment, and operational support on external security matters, including terrorism. Each member state supplies at least one person to work on the Military Staff and to maintain secure communication links with his or her national security agencies. These staff members serve a function analogous to that of the ELOs in Europol. Member states use their representatives to supply intelligence to the Military Staff and to communicate intelligence from the division to the relevant national agencies. The division then uses the intelligence shared by the member states, in addition to the intelligence gathered by Union bodies, to produce assessments for the Military Committee, the high representative for foreign policy, and other Union bodies. Another body concerned with sharing is the Situation Centre, which collects and analyzes intelligence for the high representative gathered from member states and others. Some of the Situation Centre's staff is supplied by the Intelligence Division; as of 2004 it included one staff member from seven different member states.[10]

Defection

One might agree that concerns about defection are the key barrier to intelligence sharing but conclude that the member states of the European Union estimate that their partners have few incentives to behave in such a manner. Such a conclusion has quite a bit of face validity. The fact that the member states have created and ceded a degree of authority to the European Union far greater than that of any other international organization might itself be seen as a strong indicator of high levels of mutual trust in one another's willingness to comply with the Union's policies. Furthermore, the member states face similar threats to their own security. Geographic proximity means that many member states are directly threatened by security problems at the periphery of the Union in eastern Europe, the Caucasus, and the Mediterranean. Many of them have faced or do face serious threats from domestic terrorist groups operating across borders, Islamic terror groups, and transnational organized crime. These common interests should reduce the incentives to defect, allowing intelligence to be freely shared, with little need for international institutions to monitor compliance and punish reneging.

The most direct way of determining the degree of trust among member states would be gauging their willingness to share operational intelligence. But information about the degree of sharing in actual cases is impossible for outsiders and sometimes even for the member states themselves to obtain. Security services are reluctant to divulge such information, so as to protect their sources of gathering intelligence. Furthermore, publicly available information about the degree of sharing may not be representative, as governments may be most likely to release such information only when the sharing has resulted in successful operations.

For these reasons I assess the degree to which the member states worry about defection using three indirect strategies. First, I analyze the rules about sharing for the Berne Group, Europol, and ESDP. Much more information is available about these rules than about the extent of sharing in specific cases. These rules are the product of negotiations among the governments that have agreed to share intelligence. The fact that they contain significant limitations on the degree to which participants are required to share intelligence is a good indicator that the states demanded these limits because they do in fact worry that other member states might defect. Second, I look at whether each of these institutions contains monitoring and punishment provisions that would allow those states sharing intelligence to overcome defection. Finally, I discuss public comments by decision makers that express reserve about other member states and that indicate that member states do not fully share intelligence with one another.

None of the institutions requires its members to share intelligence with one another. Instead, the decision to share is voluntary and left to the discretion of each country. The member states do not seem to have used the Berne Group to share operational intelligence. Instead, the group mainly shares ideas about effective tools and policies for countering terrorism and organized crime and how the participating services can better understand the perspectives of their counterparts. The group has no requirement or expectation that member states should share sensitive intelligence that they prefer to withhold. Gijs de Vries, the European Union's counterterrorism coordinator, admitted as much, stating that "it appears that the analysis [of the Counterterrorism Group] does not contribute much to decision-making or to the policy direction of the Union."[11] The Berne Group does plan to create a shared database on terrorism and organized crime within the next five years, but this would only "allow the collation of contextual intelligence on suspects" and "would not contain sensitive material."[12]

Europol has detailed restrictions on how its analytical files can be shared and accessed. "If an analysis is of a general nature and of a strategic type," all member states may access the report. But if it "bears on specific cases not concerning all Member States and has a direct operational aim," the only member states that can access the report are those that provided the initial information leading to the opening of the file, "those which are directly concerned by that information," and others that these member states invite to participate. Other states may learn about the existence of the analysis file through a computerized index and may request access. But the originators of the intelligence may object, in which case the Europol Convention holds that access shall be agreed by "consensus," which would seem to give these states a veto over the sharing of Europol's files. In addition, the Member State communicating an item of data to Europol shall be the sole judge of the degree of its sensitivity and variations thereof. Any dissemination or operational use of analysis data shall be decided on in consultation with the participants in the analysis. A Member State joining an analysis in progress may not, in particular, disseminate or use the data without the prior agreement of the Member States initially concerned.[13]

Member states may decline to provide intelligence to Europol if doing so involves "harming essential national security interests," "jeopardizing the success of a current investigation or the safety of individuals," or "involving information pertaining to organizations or specific intelligence activities in the field of State security."[14]

Sharing via the Military Staff's Intelligence Division has many of the same problems as the Berne Group and Europol. In particular, the Intelligence Division has no requirement that member states share intelligence that might be of value or interest to other member states or to Union institutions; rather, sharing is explicitly "voluntary." As of 2002, no arrangements were in place for sharing very secret intelligence, although one report states that most requests for information are met.[15] The division's practice of collating intelligence provided by national authorities and performing additional analysis circulated under its name means that recipients are not able to directly identify the country that provided the original information. This masking of the identity of the national sources might make those member states that are worried about security more willing to supply sensitive intelligence to the division.[16]

Full sharing, however, is difficult in practice, for two reasons. First, since only seven member states have foreign intelligence services, which vary widely in their capabilities and coverage of international developments, the recipients of shared intelligence may be able to guess the source of intelligence transmitted through the division. Second, and more important, the division receives relatively little "raw" intelligence from the member states. Instead, it relies on "finished" intelligence, which usually conceals from the recipients the most sensitive details, sources, and methods of collection. Even when the division does obtain raw or operational intelligence, it forwards only summaries to its clients.[17]

The Union also has capabilities to gather and analyze intelligence itself, although these are quite modest in comparison with those of the larger member states. The Union maintains diplomatic missions throughout the world and has special representatives assigned to specific regions, such as the Balkans, Caucasus, and the Great Lakes region of Africa, and for the Middle East peace process. These representatives are able to collect information openly from sources like government officials and publications and, through their local contacts, may occasionally obtain confidential information. They also may have detailed knowledge of specific issues and can place developments in the proper context for decision makers. But their diplomatic status means that they are not able to engage in the systematic collection or analysis of intelligence. The European Union Satellite Centre in Spain is responsible for processing and interpreting satellite images for the Union's Common Foreign and Security Policy. But the centre does not actually own or operate its own satellites. Instead, it purchases images from commercial satellites and then conducts its own analysis. This means that it does not control the satellites from which it draws images, so it cannot guarantee that relevant or timely images will be available. Furthermore, images from commercial satellites do not have the highest resolution and so are more useful as background information than as operational intelligence.[18] As one investigation reported, "Because of its largely civilian character, and the lack of enough appropriately trained staff (military image interpreters), the Torrejón Centre has difficulty in providing the virtually real time imagery necessary to the conduct of military operations during a crisis."[19]

Because the Berne Group, Europol, and the Military Staff leave it to the member states to determine what, if any, intelligence they will share with their partners, it is not surprising that none has strong or effective mechanisms for monitoring or punishing the failure to disseminate relevant intelligence or to treat shared intelligence securely. Voluntary sharing means that the receiving states have no way to ensure that a sharing state has divulged all the relevant intelligence in its possession or to determine that the intelligence has not been modified or distorted to serve the sender's interests. In principle, the assessments or work files produced by staff and liaison officers at the Berne Club, Europol, and the Military Staff could detect deliberately slanted or fabricated intelligence. Since these assessments draw from intelligence provided by all sharing states, staff and liaisons may be able to detect flaws in intelligence they receive from one national source by comparing it with by intelligence shared by others. But there is no guarantee that they will have enough high-quality intelligence from other sources in order to do this. More-over, such common assessments are not designed to determine whether a member state has withheld relevant intelligence. The Military Staff and Europol do provide some protection for the interests of sending states. The Intelligence Division of the Military Staff "cleans" shared intelligence of information that could identify its source, which gives senders some reassurance that their sources and methods of collection and analysis will not be directly revealed to other states. Europol has detailed requirements about the treatment of shared intelligence pertaining to individuals, which reassures sending states that any concerns they have about privacy rights will be respected by receiving states.

The member states' security services have managed to share intelligence successfully on numerous occasions. For example, in early 2001, European countries detected a plot by the al Qaeda terrorist network to bomb targets in Europe. Intelligence sharing allowed them to coordinate the arrest of eighteen people as well as to uncover weapons and explosives in multiple countries.[20] Despite such successes, however, politicians and officials regularly express concern that sharing is not as open as possible, and they frequently identify mistrust as the principal barrier to greater sharing. For example, after the terrorist attacks on the United States on September 11, 2001, the European Council meeting on September 21 concluded that "Member States will share with Europol, systematically and without delay, all useful data regarding terrorism."[21] Such a statement would not have been necessary if the degree of sharing was felt to be complete. British Home Secretary David Blunkett repeated this call for more open sharing of intelligence while at the same time acknowledging that Britain would not share its most sensitive intelligence, such as signals intelligence, with other member states.[22] Others observed that institutions like Europol simply could not cope with such difficulties in their present format. The director of Europol, Jürgen Storbeck, complained shortly after the attacks that each member state was still "keeping" its information "to itself" instead of sharing it with others.[23] The director of Belgium's federal police, Patrick Zanders, argued that an insufficient supply of intelligence from the member states made it difficult for Europol to respond effectively to requests for information.[24]

Similarly, after the terrorist attacks in Madrid in March 2004, ministers and senior officials stated that greater sharing would help their counterterrorism efforts but that mistrust made such sharing unlikely. France's interior minister, Nicolas Sarkozy, pointed out that strengthening the European Union's intelligence capability would be difficult because of each member state's need to protect its sources. Ireland's justice minister, Michael McDowell, who then was president of the Justice and Home Affairs Council, stated that the members had to "be realistic" in their expectations about greater sharing. Europol's Storbeck again complained that the member states did not share enough intelligence with the agency.[25] Belgium's justice minister, Laurette Onkelinx, complained that

> there are informal intelligence exchanges at the European level, both bilateral—between two states exchanging intelligence from several countries—and among all the members of what we call the Club of Berne. But this is all informal, there is no obligation, for example, to provide intelligence to a fellow member, there is no obligation to deal with such intelligence at the European level. So the idea is precisely to make such a structure formal and introduce a mandatory element into intelligence exchanges. . . . I believe that Europe must also be built on foundations of mutual confidence, otherwise there will be no sense to it.[26]

Blunkett criticized other member states, including Austria and Belgium, for proposing a new European Union intelligence agency when already many members were not living up to earlier commitments to share intelligence fully. The European Commission complained openly about the member states' "culture of secrecy" and called for greater trust to prosecute the counterterrorism campaign.[27]

Is Integration the Answer?

The member states of the European Union could benefit from more widespread sharing of intelligence. They are unwilling to move in this direction, however, because of concerns that their partners would not share fully or treat shared intelligence securely. The member states have faced similar challenges in other issue areas and have chosen to resolve them through integration. Integration involves delegating some powers to the European Union to craft policies that address the interests of all or most of the member states and then independently monitor and punish noncompliance with these policies. Integration is analytically similar to the concept of hierarchy.[28] In both integration and hierarchy, participating states voluntarily give up some autonomy in return for mutually beneficial cooperation. The Treaty of Rome, for example, created the European Commission and Court of Justice to ensure that member states abided by their obligations to implement the customs union in a nondiscriminatory manner. The treaty also designed decision-making procedures, such as voting rules in the Council of Ministers and the commission's proposal authority to make sure that resulting policy decisions reflect pan-European concerns. These policymaking and monitoring institutions allow the member states to capture the potential gains from cooperation by reducing concerns about the distributional impact of the resulting policy and possible reneging on agreements to cooperate.

Could integration also allow the member states to share intelligence more effectively? In some respects, integration seems ideally suited to resolving these difficulties. Recall from chapter 1 that states seek hierarchy when they see large possible gains from cooperation but also are concerned that their partners will defect. This accurately describes the situation here. Furthermore, creating a European body with some hierarchical elements would not be unprecedented, as other areas of cooperation in the Union contain hierarchical elements. The European Union's single currency, for example, is centrally managed by the European Central Bank, which is politically independent of the member states.

Perhaps a European intelligence organization could be created to closely monitor the collection and sharing of intelligence by national intelligence services to ensure that they are complying with obligations to provide all relevant intelligence to their counterparts. The first step would be to require member states to share relevant intelligence, rather than to allow such sharing to remain voluntary. This would ensure that member states have access to all the intelligence that their partners collect.

The second step would be to give this European agency the resources to monitor the member states' compliance with this requirement, thereby reassuring the recipients that the senders are not withholding useful intelligence and also reassuring the senders that the recipients are keeping the shared intelligence secure. Compulsory intelligence sharing would demand that the European Union have the capability to review all the intelligence that member states collect and to supervise their internal security procedures and operations.

The third step would be to create a much larger capability within the European Union to analyze the intelligence collected by the member states. As discussed earlier, some of the chief complaints about the current practice is that the intelligence shared by member states includes analysis and conclusions that focus on the concerns and interests of the sending state rather than the other member states or the Union as a whole and that shared intelligence often does not reveal the original sources of information on which the analysis is based. If the European Union had a stronger analytic capability, it would ensure that the analysis reflected the interests of the Union and all the member states and could evaluate and compare information gathered by national intelligence services. This capability might mean creating an intelligence agency within the European Union that was responsible for directly collecting and analyzing intelligence on its own, as some member states, such as Belgium and Austria, have suggested. A more modest but still substantial step in this direction would be creating a European agency that had the legal right, as well as the staff and other resources, to track and oversee intelligence developments in the member states' services. It could establish priorities for the Union for the types of intelligence that should be collected, reducing any unnecessary duplication or overlap by the member states' intelligence services. This would require the Union to be able to direct the collection and analysis by the member states' intelligence agencies, perhaps by encouraging each to specialize in particular forms of intelligence and to rely on their partners to fill in any gaps. Such an agency could make intelligence sharing more efficient by setting standards for how intelligence is collected, analyzed, distributed, and stored and what human rights and privacy rights the intelligence services must respect.

Moving toward integration would reduce some concerns about reneging and defection that have undermined attempts to expand intelligence sharing. But it also would raise new concerns about defection and how the costs and benefits of the operation of such an agency would be distributed among the member states. Although this bargaining problem has not attracted much attention to date, it probably would do so if the Union decided to integrate its member states' intelligence functions.

Three distributional problems seem likely to arise. First, each member state would want the European intelligence authority to share its perception of the most important security threats and its priorities for collecting and analyzing intelligence. Put in another way, a national government would worry that a European body might direct intelligence resources and attention away from the security issues that it found most threatening.

Second, national governments would likely have different preferences regarding the quality control, human rights, and security standards that a European body would set. Countries with a stronger tradition of protecting privacy, for example, might insist that the European Union adopt strict standards reflecting their own laws, whereas other states without such a tradition might block new standards that imposed additional burdens on their intelligence agencies. Such concerns about privacy and data protection are particularly important in the European Union, whose members have varying commitments to uphold the privacy of personal data. Human rights groups would likely object to attempts to increase intelligence sharing without addressing these concerns, on the grounds that it violated the individual rights spelled out in the European Convention on Human Rights or the treaties creating the European Union. The courts of both the Union itself and the broader convention might rule against a government's attempts to share more intelligence. The European Union could draw up new rules about the conditions under which it would share intelligence on individuals. But the negotiation over the precise content of such protections would likely reveal considerable differences among the member states. Member states less concerned about such protections might decide to restrict their sharing if strong rules were created that might compromise their ability to collect and act on intelligence. Those states attaching more importance to such rights could block more intelligence sharing until effective rules were in place.

Third, disagreements over the distribution of financial costs and benefits likely would emerge. For example, not all member states have foreign intelligence services, so would the member states with such services be expected to share all their intelligence with their European partners? If so, they might reasonably demand compensation for the costs of collecting, analyzing, and sharing such information. In addition, the larger member states might be reluctant to place their more capable intelligence services under the supervision of a European agency. These member states might expect to supply intelligence far more often than they would receive it and might worry that they would end up carrying most of the intelligence collection and analysis burden. Member states that receive intelligence from a state not belonging to the Union should be particularly concerned about defection by other member states, since countries not belonging to the Union might doubt whether the intelligence it shared would be treated securely. For example, the fact that Britain depends on intelligence it receives from the United States may make British decision makers wary of sharing it with European countries if doing so would raise questions in Washington about Britain's reliability.[29]

Creating a European intelligence body might also raise new concerns about defection. Strengthening the ability of the European Union's central institutions to oversee national intelligence collection, analysis, and sharing would require the approval of the member states' governments. But member states value their ability to make their own policies and accordingly have often prevented the transfer of additional authority to the European Union.[30] National governments that do not now trust one another enough to share intelligence fully would likely not trust sharing it with a new European institution with more intrusive powers than those of the Berne Group, Europol, and the Military Staff.

The multilateral character of the European Union also would raise the costs of detecting defection. In the European Union, much intelligence is informally shared among a few states, so that only these need to be monitored. But creating a European Union body that required intelligence to be shared would multiply the number of potentially defecting states and require that this body have comprehensive powers to monitor the activities of all the member states' intelligence agencies.

Conflicts like these have appeared in and been successfully overcome in other areas. For example, the member states expressed similar concerns when negotiating the Union's single currency. They wanted to make certain that the new monetary authority would pursue policies on inflation and growth similar to their own, create standards that would favor financial firms operating in their territory, and redistribute any funds into their national treasuries.[31] We know from past efforts at integration in Europe that overcoming these distributional conflicts is easier if one member state is willing and able to lead others to cooperate.[32] The participating member states can then adapt their intelligence and human rights standards to those of this dominant or leading state. The dominant state can also alleviate some of the political and financial costs. For instance, it can use its greater resources to establish and finance the monitoring mechanisms, such as new European institutions, needed to monitor the compliance of all member states. It can also use these resources to punish member states that renege on their promises to share intelligence and to compensate those that are likely to contribute more to the shared pool of intelligence than they receive in return.

In the first chapter I outlined the three characteristics that a state must have in order to play this leading role. First, its participation must be necessary for the integration project to succeed. This gives it the leverage, by threatening not to participate, to implement the intelligence-sharing agreement. Second, the leading state must be reasonably certain that it will benefit substantially from integration, in order to make it worthwhile to finance the monitoring and compensation required for the participation of other states. Third, it must control a disproportionate share of all the participating countries' political resources. This will enable the leading state to make credible threats to punish those states that renege on intelligence sharing by withholding benefits from cooperation on other issue areas and to compensate other states with enough money to induce them to contribute to the arrangement.

The European Union does not have a member state that meets these three criteria in the area of intelligence. The most likely candidates would be Britain, France, and Germany. The participation of all three countries is probably vital to any comprehensive intelligence-sharing arrangement. Because each has both large internal and external intelligence services that could contribute to a Europe-wide effort in this area, it would be difficult to imagine how it could succeed without the participation of all three states.

It is less clear, however, that each of these countries would gain much from participating in such an integration scheme. Britain, France, and Germany are far more capable at collecting intelligence than almost any other member state, so they would certainly be able to share much intelligence with other member states, but they may not receive much more intelligence from their partners than they do under current arrangements. Consequently, each has strong incentives to limit more intelligence sharing to only those countries inside and outside the Union that can provide a steady stream of useful information in return. Limiting the countries with which it shares intelligence would allow Britain, France, and Germany to make sure that they receive at least as much intelligence as they provide.

None of these three countries controls enough political or economic resources to lead the others. Germany's large and wealthy economy was able to dominate when the Union had fewer members and focused on economic integration. But the European Union's geographic expansion into eastern Europe and task expansion into foreign and internal security has made Germany a less crucial actor in the resulting larger and more complicated organization. No one member state, then, appears to be an obvious leader that could solve the distributional barriers to greater intelligence sharing. Leadership might be possible if some combination of the larger member states decided on common preferences and together pushed for integration in the intelligence area. But this sort of piecemeal approach is likely to take some time to spread to the European Union as a whole.

MULTISPEED COOPERATION IN THE EUROPEAN UNION

Since integration is unlikely, how could the European Union improve its intelligence sharing in other ways? What would be the implications for transatlantic cooperation on security policy?

Rather than full-scale integration or hierarchy, the Union is likely to focus its intelligence efforts on encouraging more sharing among subsets of states that have similar interests and trust one another on a particular issue or problem. Moving in this direction, however, would have many of the disadvantages that creating a more differentiated and "multispeed" European Union has in other issue areas.[33] But since the member states already are reluctant to cede even modest powers to the Union in the area of intelligence, this might be a realistic improvement over the status quo.

There already have been moves in this direction. Groups of member states with common interests now frequently meet to share intelligence on specific operations. They have made ad hoc arrangements, for example, to track terrorist groups operating within their countries. The interior ministers of Britain, France, Germany, Spain, and Italy (G5) meet regularly to discuss matters of common concern before the full meetings of the Justice and Home Affairs Council.[34] They work out agreements and bargains among themselves and then together try to persuade other member states to adopt their positions. This combined leadership is an important driver of integration. A group of states like these five, however, are less effective than a single state in the leadership role, because its members must bargain among themselves first and are unlikely to reach agreement on every issue. But this arrangement provides a forum in which to address at least some of the distributional conflicts preventing greater cooperation in intelligence. Creating more such informal bodies focused on issues of concern to a subset of member states might enable them to better understand the true interests of their partners and indirectly encourage them to share more intelligence.

One possibility is more sophisticated databases of intelligence, designed to allow a sender to post a description of each piece of intelligence in its possession. The description would have to be specific enough for prospective recipients to determine its potential value but would not contain actionable details or any information about the sources or methods by which it was obtained. Other member states could read this description and, within a short time period, request the release of the full intelligence report. This request could lead to mutually advantageous bargaining among the states, in which each could demand that the others take steps to conform with the larger political interests of them all. A sender worried about inadvertent sharing with third parties, for example, could insist that the intelligence be shared with only certain offices in the recipient's government and require the recipient to closely track dissemination of the report. Over time, successful sharing through such databases might engender greater trust among member states that regularly interact and lead to more institutionalized bilateral sharing.

Another step might be to encourage decision makers to meet with their colleagues from other member states, following the lead of the interior ministers from the G5 countries. Creating more such informal bodies focused on issues of concern to certain member states might allow them to better understand the interests of their partners and indirectly encourage them to share more intelligence. It might also lead to agreement on new policy measures by all member states. If one subset of member states were successful, others might choose to follow their lead to gain at least some influence over subsequent agreements and to ensure that they receive at least some of the advantages of cooperation.[35]

This sort of multispeed cooperation on intelligence matters would be less comprehensive or efficient than full integration. For the reasons discussed earlier, however, there are fewer barriers to its implementation. An additional advantage of multispeed cooperation is that it is adaptable to collaboration with third states, such as the United States and Canada. Multispeed cooperation, however, presents third states with a confusing patchwork of European partnerships differing in the areas they cover, their membership, and their permanence. This opacity makes it difficult for outsiders to ascertain who has authority over which functions. Accordingly, it would be much simpler for outsiders if Europe could centralize the management and oversight of intelligence, since this would present only one point of contact and negotiation. Conversely, a centralized authority might also reduce the opportunities open to outside countries. A single European Union intelligence authority would be in a stronger bargaining position to demand concessions than individual member states are. It could also reject sharing agreements that some member states might be willing to accept.

Organizing intelligence sharing along multispeed lines would be more complicated for outsiders but likely would give them more opportunities. Multispeed cooperation implies that not all member states would participate in all cooperative ventures. But it also means that third parties could be invited to join some of these ventures. For example, the United States and Canada cooperate with some but not all European countries on joint operations based on shared intelligence. Since 2002, intelligence officials from the United States, Canada, and four European countries have together operated a counterterrorist center in Paris that not only pools intelligence but also plans and coordinates operations to monitor or disrupt terror cells. The operation is headed by a French official, is funded largely by the CIA, and relies on the close cooperation of intelligence officials from the participating countries, each of whom is assigned to lead planning and implementing operations that draw on the resources of all six countries when needed.[36] This sort of flexible arrangement would be difficult to implement if the European Union had direct authority over intelligence matters. Other member states might insist on participating, which might make the United States reluctant to continue to plan such joint operations. In short, the lack of a closely coordinated intelligence apparatus in Europe offers outsiders more opportunities to join in flexible intelligence-sharing agreements.

CONCLUSIONS

The members of the European Union have good reasons to share intelligence. Common policies, including the development of a single economy and a common foreign policy, mean that the member states increasingly face similar threats to their internal and external security. It is not surprising, then, that they have established institutions like the Berne Group, Europol, and the Military Staff to facilitate the exchange of intelligence. But full and effective intelligence sharing requires that participants either trust the other participants not to defect or create rules and institutions designed to ease concerns about such defection. The available evidence indicates that mistrust is a substantial barrier to full sharing in the European Union. The member states have insisted that intelligence sharing remain voluntary, have declined to create European institutions with the capacity to monitor and punish violations of promises to share, and, in their public comments, suggest that the trust among them is too precarious to allow full sharing.

Indeed, European institutions for intelligence sharing are not designed to stop defection. Instead, their focus is on building technical mechanisms—databases, regular meetings, and liaison arrangements—that will facilitate sharing among member states. The expectation behind this approach is that member states would share a great deal of their intelligence with their partners. But because of worries about defection, the member states often do not regard the regular sharing of intelligence to be in their interest.

Such worries are not an insurmountable barrier to intelligence sharing. The United States, for example, has been able to share intelligence with countries like West Germany, South Vietnam, and Colombia, which it did not fully trust. These pairs of states managed to cooperate by creating a hierarchical relationship in which the dominant state had some direct control over its subordinate's intelligence activities in exchange for giving the subordinate political and economic benefits, subsidizing the subordinate's intelligence operations, and committing to not exploiting its dominant position.

Why, then, has the European Union not created a hierarchical structure to govern intelligence sharing among its members? The main reason is that no one member state in the Union has the desire and resources to play this dominant role. This means that the European Union has had to resort to second-best solutions to its intelligence-sharing problems. These solutions include networks of like-minded member states that have enough trust in one another and enough common interests that they can share intelligence while excluding the other member states; the possibility that a small group of more influential member states, such as the G5, would assume a leadership role in intelligence sharing; and the exchange of personnel and ideas with the goal of creating mutual trust and a better understanding of the other member states' interests and concerns. Over the long term, these efforts may succeed in encouraging member states to share more intelligence with one another but are unlikely to do so as quickly or as effectively as would the creation of a more centralized authority.

One of the United States' top foreign policy priorities is countering Islamic terrorism, especially the al Qaeda network and those groups inspired by or collaborating with it. Accurate intelligence is crucial to this effort. Even the most effective terrorist groups, like al Qaeda, control far fewer resources than do the states against which they direct their violence. It is this asymmetry in resources that leads them to adopt the tactic of terrorist attacks, which by randomly targeting civilians gives them the initiative and attracts more attention to their grievances. This asymmetry also leads terrorist groups to devote a great deal of attention to concealing from state authorities their membership, sources of finance, training locations, and communications. Accurate intelligence, however, allows the government to use its police, military, and other resources to disrupt a terrorist group's activities. As Derek Reveron put it, "The war on terror requires high levels of intelligence to identify a threat relative to the amount of force required to neutralize it. This fact elevates intelligence in importance and places it on the frontline against terrorism."[1]

Intelligence is most useful for those elements of a counterterrorism policy intended to disrupt such groups' recruitment, financing, security of operations, bases, movement of personnel, and so on, through the actions of the state's military, police, intelligence, and judiciary. Intelligence also is very useful for internal or homeland security if it can identify likely targets that should be better protected against attack. Operational intelligence is less important to policies aimed at reducing support for terrorist groups by, for example, promoting economic development or democracy. But analysis that draws on secret intelligence might help decision makers better implement such policies by, for example, accurately specifying the grievances that motivate terrorist groups and their supporters.

Al Qaeda's objectives and organization make it a uniquely dangerous terrorist foe and one on which it is exceptionally difficult to collect accurate and useful intelligence. It has demonstrated its willingness and ability to launch high-casualty attacks within the United States and against American interests abroad. It sponsors or supports local terrorist movements or insurgencies around the world, including those in Algeria, Egypt, Iraq, Afghanistan, India, Indonesia, and Russia. Al Qaeda carefully selects members of high intelligence and initiative from many nationalities, enabling the organization to lead and work with local recruits in many parts of the world; to undertake complex, carefully planned, and long-term missions; and to study and learn from its own experiences as well as those of other terrorist groups. Al Qaeda has the ability to adapt successfully to unforeseen developments. It frequently changes the means by which it communicates information to operatives and has maintained its planning and operations despite losing its base in Afghanistan in late 2001. And it devotes a great deal of energy to maintaining its operational security.[2]

The fact that al Qaeda is a transnational group makes thwarting it even more difficult. Al Qaeda has proved to be a terrorist organization of truly global reach, having launched attacks in dozens of countries. It has members and supporters in even more countries, giving it numerous sources of funds and recruits and multiple locations for organizing, training, and hiding its members. These countries include those with weak or failed governments, which are unable to fight back against the group, as well as those with powerful political elements that share some of al Qaeda's objectives and thus are unwilling to oppose it. Al Qaeda's transnational scope has led it to adopt a less hierarchical organizational form than that of many other terrorist groups. This means that eliminating one or a few leaders of the organization in one location will not seriously disrupt the ability of branches in other locations to continue operating.[3]

Al Qaeda's transnational organization also means that other countries can contribute intelligence on it that the United States would find costly or impossible to collect on its own. Not surprisingly, those countries in which al Qaeda operates almost always are in a better position to collect "human intelligence" from defectors or agents. A common criticism of the United States' intelligence community is that it devotes too many resources to the collection and analysis of more technical forms of intelligence gathered, for example, from advanced satellites or communication interception systems. Other governments rely more heavily on the collection of human intelligence and often have a cadre of trained intelligence personnel that are natives in the linguistic and cultural environment in which al Qaeda operates in their country. This allows them to make connections with potential informants more easily and to place the intelligence provided by such informants in the appropriate context. Consequently, countries in western Europe, North Africa, the Persian Gulf, and South and Southeast Asia are able to collect intelligence that the United States cannot and thus are in a position to share their intelligence with the United States for their mutual benefit.[4]

Some of these states, however, also have powerful reasons to renege on their promises to share intelligence with the United States. For instance, European governments face legal challenges to some of their foreign intelligence activities. Domestic political pressures have prompted some states in the Middle East and Europe to curtail their collaboration with the United States. Religious or nationalist groups or elements of the government apparatus in some countries are less enthusiastic about taking action against al Qaeda. Governments may have conflicting interests with the United States on other issues that have caused them to minimize their cooperation on counterterrorism. Even allies of the United States may refuse to take action against al Qaeda in order to avoid retaliation by the group. Some countries have poorly developed or corrupt police, judicial, and intelligence bureaucracies that are unable to take such effective action in the first place. Still other governments may wish to exaggerate the effectiveness of their action against, and the accuracy of their intelligence on, al Qaeda in order to win the United States' approval and support.[5]

The problem for the United States is that some of the countries that have the most valuable intelligence on al Qaeda are also those with the strongest incentives to defect from agreements to share such intelligence, and such defection is very difficult to detect. This inconsistency has attracted considerable attention from those with an interest in improving their counterterrorism policy. Most counsel that the optimal solution is to reduce reliance on shared intelligence and to build the United States' capacity to independently collect and analyze intelligence on Islamic terrorism. This view takes seriously the problem of monitoring for defection in an anarchic international system. It has concluded that the safest policy is to limit intelligence sharing to trustworthy states and to strengthen national intelligence-gathering capabilities on issues for which such states are in short supply.[6]

Yet the United States has managed to strengthen intelligence-sharing arrangements with many of these countries. How, if at all, do such arrangements address concerns about defection? At one extreme, arranging effective intelligence sharing with countries that have the fewest incentives to defect, such as those in western Europe, has been rather straightforward. In many (but not all) areas, the United States and Europe have developed mechanisms for the regular exchange of intelligence.

At the other extreme, the United States has usually not shared intelligence with countries that have the strongest motives to defect, such as Iran and Syria. These outcomes are understandable based on the trust-based and liberal institutionalist explanations of cooperation. Although Iran and Syria undoubtedly have intelligence that would be of value to the U.S. counterterrorism policies, American officials have little confidence that these governments could be trusted to share their intelligence reliably and honestly, and so they do not share intelligence. In contrast, European governments have the fewest incentives to defect and so are trusted by the United States to share their intelligence reliably. This initial trust is has been reinforced through bargaining strategies and some third-party monitoring of compliance, primarily through media investigations, legislative oversight, and the activities of human rights groups.

More difficult to explain are the arrangements with such countries as Egypt and Jordan, which are among the United States' most important counterterrorism intelligence partners but also face substantial pressures to renege. Cooperation with these states therefore is not based on trust or the precepts of liberal institutionalism. Indeed, mutual trust is not nearly as strong here as it is in relations between the United States and European countries, and third-party monitoring strategies linked to reputation are difficult to implement in their closed societies. The solution has been hierarchical intelligence-sharing relationships that give the United States some ability to directly monitor and control its partners' intelligence activities. This gives the United States a way to obtain intelligence from partners of questionable reliability by directly monitoring their compliance. The United States has also been able to use its greater political, economic, and military power to manage its hierarchical relations with these countries. In return for their being more effective counterterrorism allies, it gives its intelligence partners political support, economic aid, and military and intelligence training. But this aid also helps reinforce the hierarchical relations by giving the United States leverage that it can threaten to use in case of defection and by providing multiple channels through which American counterterrorism agencies can monitor their partners in other countries.

The relational contracting explanation of intelligence sharing shows how the United States has been able to share intelligence with states that it fears would defect from more traditional, arm's-length arrangements. It also suggests new ways of thinking about intelligence reform in the United States. Many prescriptions for intelligence reform advocate that American intelligence agencies develop a more robust human intelligence collection capacity. A key rationale for this suggestion is that many other states cannot be trusted to share the relevant human intelligence that they collect. But a focus on hierarchy indicates that the United States does not have to base its evaluations of other states' contributions to its intelligence needs solely on their trustworthiness; instead, it can replace trust with hierarchy. Advocates of intelligence reform thus have overstated the costs and risks of relying on partner states to share intelligence.

Sharing Intelligence on Islamic Terrorism

Anarchic Sharing: Europe

Western Europe and Canada can share much useful intelligence with the United States and have relatively few incentives to defect. The foreign intelligence services of Britain, France, Germany, and a few other countries can collect information overseas and share it with the United States. British and French intelligence are particularly strong in the Arab world and South Asia. The fact that western Europe serves as a base and target for al Qaeda and related Islamic terrorist groups means that domestic intelligence and law enforcement agencies also can supply the United

States with valuable intelligence. It also means that the United States can give these governments intelligence it obtains elsewhere, which then may use domestic law enforcement to monitor or detain suspected terrorists.

For the most part, western European countries have few incentives to renege on the counterterrorism intelligence it shares with the United States. Governments in this region clearly feel vulnerable to attack by Islamic terrorist groups. Britain and Spain have suffered major attacks, and Germany, Italy, Denmark, and other countries have discovered groups planning attacks. Countering Islamic terrorism therefore is a political priority for both the United States and the European Union.[7] Even the opposition of Germany, France, and other countries to the American invasion of Iraq in 2003 has not diminished this interest in working with the United States to counter al Qaeda and related groups.

These interests have led European countries to regularly share analysis and operational intelligence with the United States. For its part, the United States has little incentive to add hierarchy to those elements of the relationship that do not raise human rights questions. Instead, the United States and Europe have been able to trust each other to share a great deal of intelligence without direct oversight or monitoring of how the intelligence is collected and analyzed. American intelligence agencies also maintain regular contact with their counterparts in Europe; analysts from European countries often meet with their American counterparts; and the CIA and FBI have liaison offices in many European countries that devote much of their time to sharing intelligence. Much transatlantic intelligence is shared in many areas. The United States has access to the law enforcement and intelligence data and analysis on terrorism maintained by the European Union's European Police Agency (Europol), and Europol and the United States have liaison officers to facilitate the exchange of information. They also regularly compare and discuss their assessments of the threats posed by various terrorist groups.[8] Member states use NATO to exchange threat assessments and analysis as well as operational intelligence related to the alliance's peacekeeping operations in Afghanistan.[9]

It is unusual for states to share intelligence with many others. Compared with bilateral sharing, the greater number of partners makes it difficult to evaluate the accuracy of the received intelligence and to control the dissemination of intelligence shared with others.[10] The fact that the

United States and European states rely on multinational mechanisms to share intelligence on terrorism indicates that they have relatively few concerns about defection. At the same time, it is important not to read too much into the practice of multinational intelligence sharing, as there is little public evidence about precisely what intelligence the participating countries share. Their multinational sharing may well be limited largely to intelligence of less operational value and to less sensitive analysis of trends in terrorism.

We know that intelligence shared across the Atlantic has allowed governments to uncover terrorist activities and to interdict plans to launch attacks, although the authorities will not release many details about such cooperation. For example, the United States has shared intercepted telephone calls and e-mail messages with German and Danish intelligence and law enforcement agencies, allowing them to arrest Islamist militants planning terrorist attacks.[11] Italian officials allowed the Federal Bureau of Investigation (FBI) to question a suspected terrorist about links to terrorist activities in the United States.[12] France provided the United States with intelligence that helped convict individuals accused of planning major terrorist attacks.[13] In closing down a plot to bomb transatlantic airliners flying from London, the British government shared intelligence on the plot with the FBI, which followed up on leads in the United States.[14]

After each successful attack, authorities from many countries now meet on short notice to share intelligence in the hope of catching the perpetrators and learning about the terrorists' operations and tactics. After the major terrorist attacks in Madrid in 2004 and London in 2005, both the Spanish and British governments enlisted the help of United States and other European countries. In turn, these countries offered the intelligence they had that was relevant to the investigations, used intelligence provided by the Spanish and British to investigate their own residents' links to the attacks, and learned about the attackers' motivations, international links, and tactics from the local governments' investigations of the attacks.[15] Furthermore, there is some evidence that the United States and certain European allies undertake joint operations based on shared intelligence. Since 2002, intelligence officials from the United States, France, and four other countries have together operated a counterterrorist center in Paris that not only pools intelligence but also plans and coordinates operations to monitor or disrupt terrorist cells. The operation is headed by a French official, is funded largely by the

CIA, and relies on close cooperation among intelligence officials from the participating countries, each of whom is assigned to take the lead in planning and implementing operations that draw on the resources of all six countries when needed.[16]

European governments do face pressure not to share intelligence with the United States in cases involving violations of human rights. Europe has a highly developed set of human rights law, robust international monitoring and enforcement through domestic legal processes as well the European Court of Human Rights and, on some issues, the European Union, along with politically important domestic constituents that place a high priority on compliance with these laws. Human rights concerns have made it more difficult for European governments to cooperate with the United States on certain practices concerning the detention and treatment of suspected terrorists and the sharing of personal data. An important objective of U.S. counterterrorism policy has been to kill or capture and interrogate senior al Qaeda members and other Islamic terrorist leaders. In many cases this goal can be met only with the active cooperation, or at least the acquiescence, of those states in which the suspects circulate. Cooperation with these policies has been controversial in Europe. Many object to the treatment of detainees in facilities under American control in Guantánamo Bay, Afghanistan, Iraq, and secret prisons elsewhere. Transatlantic tension has been strongest on issues that directly involve European countries' territory or residents. These include the extrajudicial detention by the United States of suspects in Europe and their transferal or "rendition" elsewhere (one report estimates that this has been done more than one hundred times), the use of landing facilities in Europe on more than twelve hundred occasions to transport suspects to third countries, and secret, American-run prisons believed to be located in countries in eastern Europe that have recently joined the European Union.[17]

This opposition has posed fewer problems for the United States than many people assume. Some governments seem to have cooperated initially with American operations to detain individuals on their territory. The widely discussed American abduction of Abu Omar in Italy and his rendition to Egypt required some cooperation from the Italian intelligence service. Many European governments allowed U.S. intelligence to use their airspace and airports to transport suspects. It is unclear if security agencies in Europe were aware of the full extent of the United States' rendition operation. But cases such as those in Italy and elsewhere should have alerted them to what was happening. The ability of citizens and journalists to later unearth and map the flight plans of many rendition flights indicates that it would not have been too difficult for European governments to grasp the scope of the program if they had been interested in doing so.[18]

American intelligence also was able to run secret prisons in the region with at least the tacit support of the host countries' governments. It was only when this became public and threatened to expose governments to legal and political sanctions that the Europeans began complaining loudly and backing away from cooperation. Note, too, that European governments do not object to the detention of all potential terrorists, only the extrajudicial detention of such suspects. In fact, many European countries have changed their laws to give authorities greater power to detain suspected terrorists. In some cases in which an individual was sought by several political jurisdictions, the countries involved have handed him over to the country with the most stringent limits on the suspect's rights.[19]

Data protection laws have impeded, but not prevented, the sharing of personal data with the United States. European governments and firms regularly collect two types of personal data of interest to the United States—the names of passengers traveling on international airline flights and data on international financial transfers. Airlines collect passenger name records (PNRs) to facilitate the exchange of information on passengers using multiple carriers for the same trip. All PNRs include such basic details as the passenger's name, contact information, and itinerary. Many airlines also include additional personal information such as passport details, date and place of birth, payment details, and emergency contacts. After the September 11 attacks, American intelligence agencies asked airlines to provide archived PNRs as well as current records before the departure of flights to the United States. But the distribution of information in PNRs is restricted by the European Union's data protection laws, which prohibit the sharing of personal data with countries, such as the United States, that lack comparable data protection standards. Officials of the European Union, which determines third countries' compliance with this standard on behalf of its member states, worried that the European Court of Justice would overturn a decision to share PNRs with the United States. In 2001 the Union agreed to share these data with the United States for two years, during which they negotiated to bring American treatment of PNRs up to European standards. The two sides reached a temporary agreement in 2003 and a permanent arrangement the next year. As feared, however, the European Court of Justice did invalidate this agreement in 2006, forcing the United States and European Union to renegotiate portions of the agreement in 2007.[20]

Similar concerns did not prevent Belgium from sharing financial intelligence with the United States. Brussels is the headquarters of the Society for Worldwide Interbank Financial Telecommunication (SWIFT), which allows thousands of banks and other financial institutions around the world to securely exchange messages regarding financial transfers. SWIFT managers secretly granted the United States access to these messages after the September 11 attacks. But they soon became uneasy about the legal basis of the cooperation and persuaded the United States to limit its searches, to hire an independent auditing firm to ensure that the data be used only for terrorism investigations, and to allow them to veto intelligence searches they considered inappropriate. After details of this cooperation became public in 2006, privacy bodies in Belgium and the European Union ruled that it violated the Union's data protection rules. Few political leaders in Europe, however, were willing to advocate a stop to the sharing of data with the United States. Indeed, most European governments very likely were aware of this arrangement before 2006, as SWIFT management had informed the European Central Bank and the national central banks of many western European countries of its cooperation with the United States. It was only after the program became public and attracted the criticism of data protection organizations and human rights groups that they felt the need to place the program on a secure legal foundation. The European Union and United States worked out an arrangement in which SWIFT could continue to share financial information with U.S. government agencies certified as having privacy protections equivalent to the European Union's more stringent standards.[21]

From the American perspective, the human rights concerns of some western European states were a form of defection from the expectations that the two sides would share intelligence for counterterrorism purposes. Why, then, did the United States not seek to create a hierarchical relationship to prevent this? The answer is that the benefits it would have received were not worth it. The costs of hierarchy would have been substantial, since some European countries, like Britain, France, and Germany, already had considerable economic and military resources. Because the United States had a strong desire to share intelligence with the European countries, they would have been in a good position to demand considerable compensation for accepting direct oversight of some of their intelligence activities.

At the same time, the benefits of hierarchical control would have been modest because the differences in policy between the United States and most European countries were actually rather small. In principle, the European governments did not object to sharing this information with the United States, but they wanted to make sure that the United States would not abuse the information in ways that would intrude on individual privacy. This gap proved reasonably easy to bridge, which meant that it was more constructive for the United States to work out formal agreements with European countries rather than seek hierarchical control over their intelligence activities. The United States eventually negotiated an agreement on PNRs that satisfied the European Union, and the Union allowed their airlines to share their PNRs with the United States while these negotiations were taking place. The European governments also acquiesced to the sharing of SWIFT messages with the United States and, when it become public, moved quickly to place this program on a proper legal footing.

Negotiated solutions for the treatment of detainees were more problematic. One reason was that some of the United States' activities, such as detaining people without a court order, sending suspects to countries whose security services would mistreat them, and interrogating prisoners using torture, violated European human rights. European governments would have faced powerful complaints from domestic and international courts had they cooperated with these activities. Recognizing this, the United States altered its practices so that they did not need the cooperation of European intelligence and law enforcement. The United States stopped illegally detaining individuals in Europe, stopped using European airports to transport suspects, and closed down the secret prisons believed to be located in eastern Europe. These changes made it somewhat more difficult, but not impossible, for the United States to continue to treat suspects as it had in the past. In other words, once European governments began complaining about the treatment of detainees, the United States could pursue its policy on its own at a much lower cost than that of exercising hierarchical control.

Hierarchical Sharing: Morocco, Jordan, and Egypt

Although Morocco, Jordan, and Egypt can offer valuable intelligence, they also are likely to renege promises to share it fully with the United States. The United States has tried to mitigate this inclination to defect by creating hierarchical intelligence-sharing relationships. Countries that clearly fall into this category include Egypt, Jordan, and Morocco. Pakistan also has agreed to some elements of hierarchy in its intelligence relationship with the United States but in general has more strongly resisted American efforts to exert more direct control over its intelligence agencies.

The United States can obtain two types of valuable intelligence from these countries. Many members, sympathizers, and financiers of Islamic terrorist groups live in or are citizens of these countries. Local intelligence services have the requisite staff, cultural and linguistic knowledge, and legal (and often extralegal) authority to collect intelligence on these individuals. Furthermore, none of these countries is a democracy, and all use repression and coercion to maintain the government's hold on power. Their intelligence services are known to use torture and other harsh techniques to interrogate detainees. Nonetheless, American authorities believe that this is useful for their "extraordinary rendition" of suspected terrorists. The United States arranges for the transport of suspected terrorists detained in third countries to Jordan, Egypt, Morocco, and a few other countries for questioning, with the knowledge that interrogators will not hesitate to engage in human rights abuses, such as torture or threats against detainees' families, to obtain intelligence.

Even though the United States values intelligence sharing with these countries, it also worries that each has reasons why it may not share fully. Government agencies, including those involved in internal security, in all these countries are known for corruption.[22] This may deter officials from pursuing or interrogating terrorist suspects aggressively; indeed, such suspects may be able to pay bribes in order to avoid capture and interrogation. American intelligence agencies also suspect that some of the people working in intelligence and internal security may sympathize with the objectives and actions of Islamic terrorist groups.[23]

The basic ideology and many of the leaders of al Qaeda were originally from Egypt, where for decades they struggled to overthrow its secular governments. Al Qaeda and related groups also have drawn considerable support from individuals in North Africa, including Morocco and

Moroccans living in western Europe. Jordan has not generated as much popular support for Islamic terrorism, although the government worries about the development of stronger indigenous terrorists linked to al Qaeda. Finally, American officials have worried for well over a decade that Pakistan's principal intelligence agency, Inter-Service Intelligence (ISI) retains ties to al Qaeda and the Taliban.[24] Moreover, the domestic political climate may cause these governments to avoid taking strong action against terrorist movements. Indeed, there is some evidence that although all these governments see Islamic terrorism as directly threatening their continued rule and share the desire of the United States to try to defeat the movement, their publics nonetheless support the movement's chief political complaints and some of its objectives. In addition, they oppose the United States' policies in the Middle East.[25] Concerns about internal politics thus sometimes persuades even autocratic governments not to share all their intelligence on terrorist activities with the United States in order to avoid alienating their domestic supporters.

The political situation in Egypt, Jordan, and Morocco has allowed these countries, however, to create hierarchical relationships with the United States that benefit both parties. Even though elements in all these countries are sympathetic to al Qaeda or oppose cooperation with the United States, the governments do not share these views. Each government feels acutely threatened by the activities of al Qaeda and the broader jihadist movement. These movements have targeted governments in the region for obstructing the achievement of their political objectives and for allying with the United States and consequently have declared as one of the main goals their overthrow and replacement with Islamist governments.

All these countries have been targets of attacks carried out by or inspired by al Qaeda, and the governments regard residents who support or sympathize with al Qaeda as powerful threats to their hold on office. Thus there are few political differences between the official policy of governments in the region and the United States regarding the importance of undermining Islamic terrorist movements. This common goal reassures these governments that they can cede some of their authority over intelligence matters to the United States, which has less incentive to exploit this authority for its own objectives. The creation of hierarchical intelligence-sharing relationships is also aided by the fact that most of these governments have close security ties to the United

States. These ties provide convenient paths through which the United States can indirectly reward its clients for cooperating on intelligence, for example, through increases in foreign or military aid. At the same time, the intelligence-sharing relationship can be shaped so that the hierarchical relationship with the United States is hidden from public view. The management of extraordinary rendition is a good example of this. Governments release very little information about what suspects they have in custody through this program or how they are treated. This secrecy prevents al Qaeda from learning what intelligence the governments have obtained from suspects. It also reduces the visibility of the subordination to the United States, which likely minimizes the backlash that might arise if more details were made public.

The United States has used the three mechanisms discussed in chapter 1—financing, oversight, and training—to control and monitor these states. The United States provides substantial foreign and military assistance to all three countries, and they also are among the largest recipients of U.S. military training. Each year, dozens to hundreds of military and intelligence personnel from each country visit the United States for training, and more receive instruction from American personnel in their home countries. Such training, especially in Egypt and Morocco, likely covers dealing with internal security and counterterrorism. Furthermore, since September 11, the United States has developed new, similar training programs that focus specifically on intelligence and counterterrorism and face fewer legal limitations on personnel from countries with poor human rights records.[26]

The United States also is reported to have directly subsidized Jordan's and Egypt's intelligence agencies.[27] In exchange, American officials are closely involved in the treatment and interrogation of individuals transported to these countries for interrogation. Reports suggest that these interrogations are actually conducted by local personnel, many of whom have linguistic skills and cultural backgrounds similar to those of the suspects. But American intelligence officials help select which individuals will be interrogated, provide many of the questions to be asked, and closely monitor and supervise the detainees' questioning and treatment. Some American intelligence personnel appear to have essentially permanent positions and play an active role in Jordan's intelligence agency.[28]

This division of labor—with Americans identifying suspects, guiding the interrogations, and integrating the intelligence obtained with other sources, and local authorities taking responsibility for the suspects' actual detention and interrogation—serves two purposes. It maximizes the mutual gains available from cooperation by drawing on the strengths of each state. The United States contributes suspects and questions and analysis drawn from its more wide-ranging sources of information on Islamic terrorism, and the host government provides personnel with the linguistic skills to conduct interrogations and a willingness to violate international human rights norms concerning the treatment of detainees.

But the same sharing of responsibility also gives the subordinate states some leverage over the United States. They detain the suspected terrorists on their territory and give the Americans access to the results of their interrogations and thus could withhold intelligence by stopping their questioning or limiting the Americans' access and participation. These subordinate states must worry also that the United States might decide not to share intelligence. For example, the Americans' emphasis might shift from Islamic terrorism to other threats, making the United States less willing to provide financing and training. Or the subordinate states could worry that investigations by the media or the U.S. Congress might reveal details of their participation with the United States in intelligence gathering. Such revelations could strengthen opposition to these regimes by Islamic terrorist groups or even their own citizens. By giving them some power to harm the United States, a division of labor may reassure the subordinate states that they are not entirely at the dominant state's mercy. At the same time, the United States does limit its exposure to such defection by not relying on these states to interrogate the suspects. The most senior al Qaeda suspects are detained and interrogated by American personnel in sites that are entirely under U.S. control in Afghanistan, Poland, and Romania. Less important suspects are subject to rendition to countries in the region. This division of responsibility may reflect concerns about the reliability of Jordan, Egypt, and Morocco to keep secure the more valuable intelligence that these suspects could convey to their captors.[29]

The United States has tried to create a hierarchical intelligence-sharing relationship with Pakistan as well, but the Pakistani government has resisted because of domestic political concerns. Sharing intelligence with Pakistan is very important to the United States. The most senior al Qaeda leaders operate from this country, and the Pakistani ISI is in a good position to collect intelligence on their location and activities. Moreover, many terrorist cells in other parts of the world have links to al Qaeda that run through Pakistan, so collecting intelligence there might even be able to thwart attacks planned overseas.[30]

While the potential benefits of intelligence cooperation with Pakistan are likely higher than with any other country, the risks to the United States of the Pakistanis' defection also are very high. Its government clearly sees al Qaeda as a serious threat to its security, giving it powerful reasons to cooperate with the United States. At the same time, however, important forces oppose such cooperation or make it difficult for the country's political leadership to translate its desire for cooperation into practice. Elements of the ISI and armed forces are believed to sympathize with al Qaeda and/or the Taliban.[31] This sympathy, along with widespread corruption, may reduce Pakistan's willingness to share intelligence on these groups or to act on intelligence provided by the United States. Furthermore, an abundance of political issues prevent the military and intelligence services from focusing on collecting intelligence against al Qaeda. These include the prospect of armed conflict with India, disagreements over the services' role in internal politics, and maintenance of the military's political status during the great political instability after 2001.[32]

The absence of much domestic political support for close cooperation with the United States or for the use of military force within Pakistan in counterterrorist operations further reduces the government's incentives to collect or to share intelligence. Such pressures are demonstrated, for example, in the Pakistani government's attempts to manage the country's tribal areas. The Pakistani government has never had full control over these areas, which border Afghanistan and are believed to be where surviving leaders of al Qaeda have their bases of operation. The Pakistani government has resisted American pressure to take aggressive action in this area. In fact, in recent years, it has actually reduced its military and intelligence presence in the region, hoping that respect for local tribal governance would lead the population to stop offering refuge to al Qaeda and the Taliban. American officials cite Pakistan's policy as the main reason for the continued survival of these movements.[33]

The outcome of these conflicting pressures within Pakistan has been a struggle with the United States over the nature and extent of intelligence sharing. The United States has offered Pakistan considerable inducements in exchange for more closely directing and monitoring its efforts to collect or to act on intelligence on al Qaeda, including large sums of money, weapons and training for the Pakistani military, and support for the military government that ruled the country until 2008.[34] But the Pakistani government has rejected many of these efforts. For example, since 2001 Pakistan has been one of the world's largest recipients of U.S. aid, much of which is directly tied to the country's efforts against al Qaeda. Pakistan also has been the largest beneficiary by far of the United States' Coalition Support Fund, which has been used to reward or compensate countries for assisting with specific American counterterrorism operations. This fund, which requires recipients to document their support, gives the United States an important source of detailed information on Pakistan's counterterrorism and intelligence actions. But Pakistan does not provide the United States with enough information for American to evaluate its performance. The United States has been reluctant to insist that Pakistan's reimbursements be clearly linked to its performance, fearing that doing so would alienate the country and reduce its interest in cooperating.[35]

The United States and Pakistan also regularly disagree on how to collect and use actionable intelligence on the activities of al Qaeda or the Taliban. The United States has urged that its large military operation in Afghanistan be granted some rights to cross into Pakistan to collect or act on such intelligence. But the Pakistani government has refused, presumably fearing that American military action on its territory might complicate its authority in the border regions or further inflame domestic opposition to cooperation with the United States.[36] Pakistan's unwillingness either to take actions that will make it more trustworthy to the United States or to subordinate itself to American intelligence has led the United States to develop its own substantial autonomous intelligence capabilities in the region. These include intelligence functions attached to the American military effort in Afghanistan, the introduction of more undercover American agents in Pakistan to collect human intelligence, and attempts to collect intelligence from satellites and communication intercepts independent of the Pakistani intelligence services.[37]

Little Sharing: Syria and Iran

Some countries have intelligence of value to the United States in its campaign against Islamic terrorism and also are likely to defect, but for which a hierarchical intelligence-sharing relationship would be too costly to develop or maintain. Syria and Iran fit into this category, as both have valuable intelligence. Syria is an important transit point for foreign fighters and funds going to support al Qaeda's activities in Iraq. Many individuals that held prominent positions in the administration of former Iraqi dictator Saddam Hussein now live in exile in Syria, and some may have connections to insurgents operating against the United States in Iraq. Because the Syrian and Iranian governments actively collect human intelligence on developments in Iraq, they likely have sources of information that are beyond the reach of American intelligence and that would be useful to the U.S. military and political missions there. Iran also operates political and intelligence missions in Afghanistan that could provide useful intelligence to the United States. Some important members of al Qaeda are believed to reside in Iran, although it is not clear how much the Iranian government controls their activities and contacts overseas. These individuals may well have information about the group's activities that would interest the United States.

Profound policy differences, of course, are the major barrier preventing these countries from sharing such intelligence with the United States and keeping the United States from trusting the content of any information these countries would share. The United States and Syria differ over the latter's relationship with Israel, intervention in Lebanon, and possible support of insurgents in Iraq. American relations with Iran are troubled by accusations that Iran is developing nuclear weapons, supports terrorism, and intervenes in Iraqi and Afghan politics in ways that counteract U.S. efforts in these countries. The fact that these differences influence each country's core interests in the region and beyond makes hierarchy too expensive a solution to the problem of defection. The United States would have to make major policy sacrifices in order for either Syria or Iran to allow it to supervise their intelligence activities. Conversely, such supervision would make these countries very vulnerable to American defection in the form of interfering in their internal political affairs or their ability to collect intelligence overseas.

It is not surprising, then, that intelligence has been shared with Iran or Syria only infrequently, when the countries perceive that they face an immediate threat in common with the United States. Such cooperation has not been sustained beyond these shared threats, nor does it appear to have been institutionalized in formal sharing arrangements laying out expectations about what intelligence each state would be expected to provide. Syria did share considerable intelligence on al Qaeda shortly after the September 11 attacks, apparently because the government saw al Qaeda as a threat to its position and out of a desire to avoid a confrontation with the United States. American intelligence agencies also used their practice of extraordinary rendition to deliver suspected terrorists to Syria for questioning by the authorities, who shared the evidence gathered in these interrogations with the United States. But this cooperation seems to have ended sometime around 2003 owing to Syria's opposition to the invasion of Iraq and conflicts over its actions in neighboring Lebanon. Iran also has shared intelligence with the United States, especially on individuals connected to al Qaeda who fled to Iran after the American invasion of Afghanistan in 2001, as well as on developments in that country. But more recent conflicts with Iran over nuclear energy and Iraq may well have reduced Iran's willingness to continue sharing intelligence.

CONCLUSIONS

American counterterrorism policy can benefit substantially from sharing intelligence with other states. But it cannot trust all of them to keep this intelligence secure or to hand over all the relevant intelligence they could collect. The United States can compensate for this lack of trust by negotiating hierarchical relationships to govern intelligence sharing. Hierarchy allows the United States to limit these states' decision-making autonomy by directly monitoring their compliance with their commitment to share intelligence.

Creating hierarchies is expensive for the United States, which in return must offer material rewards and credible guarantees that it will not exploit its influence. Thus, according to the third expectation developed in chapter 1, when the United States has sufficient trust in another state that it estimates the probability of defection to be low, hierarchy offers too few benefits to justify these costs. This is essentially the situation with sharing intelligence with Europe. The United States knows that European countries want to combat Islamic terrorism and thus generally perceive sharing intelligence with the United States to be in their interest. There thus is little need to create a hierarchy to govern these relationships.

Hierarchy is, however, a worthwhile option when the partner state has strong incentives to renege on its promise to share and when the dominant state can oversee its activities for an acceptable cost in accordance with the third relational contracting expectation developed in chapter 1. Examples of this arrangement include Jordan, Egypt, and Morocco. All three are allies of the United States and are committed to countering Islamic terrorism but face political and administrative pressures to renege on this commitment. The United States has been able to minimize such reneging by developing means of controlling and monitoring these subordinate states in exchange for security commitments, financial assistance, and control mechanisms permitting the subordinate states to retain some autonomy. Hierarchical relationships are too expensive, however, for relations with other states, such as Iran and Syria, that have intelligence of value to the United States but do not share its political goals.

Successful intelligence sharing with European countries and the absence of sharing with states such as Iran and Syria can be explained by mutual trust and liberal institutionalism. Iran and Syria have many foreign-policy interests that conflict sharply with the priorities of the United States. These conflicting interests make it very difficult for these governments to trust each other to share intelligence fully and reliably. This mutual mistrust, then, is sufficient to explain the absence of cooperation in these cases.

The United States' recent experience of sharing intelligence with European countries also is consistent with these explanations. Because the United States and countries in Europe all view al Qaeda and related movements as serious threats to their security, they therefore have a strong interest in sharing intelligence related to terrorist activities. Unusual for intelligence sharing, this cooperation also has been supported by some of the institutional arrangements identified by liberal institutionalism. The fact that all these countries are democracies with a free press and independent judicial and legislative branches means that journalists, judges, and/or legislators will conduct independent third-party investigations that will reveal information about compliance with promises to share intelligence.[38]

But mutual trust and liberal institutionalism cannot account for the successful sharing of intelligence with countries like Jordan, Morocco, and Egypt. The governments of these countries have powerful incentives not to share intelligence with the United States, leading to an absence of strong mutual trust. But these countries have managed to overcome this and to share intelligence, by constructing hierarchical relationships that give the United States the tools and authority to supervise some of its partners' intelligence activities in exchange for political, diplomatic, and economic assistance. Explanations of cooperation based on trust or liberal institutionalism cannot be used for such relationships because they assume that international politics is always characterized by anarchic relations between independent states. The relational contracting approach to international politics relaxes this assumption and theorizes the conditions under which hierarchy will materialize in international politics, as well as how it can alleviate concerns about defection. The application of this approach to intelligence sharing sheds new light on the conditions under which states can share intelligence for counterterrorism purposes.

At the same time, though, we need to be careful in drawing causal inferences from the cases presented in this chapter. These contemporary cases have two methodological weaknesses compared with those analyzed in earlier chapters. First, the historical cases analyzed in chapters 2 and 3 drew on a large stock of declassified documents that facilitated fine-grained process tracing, whereas most of the internal documents concerning counterterrorism remain classified. I have thus drawn heavily on investigations and reports produced by journalists, nongovernmental organizations, and national legislatures. These accounts may contain a systematic bias in the facts that they report or be incomplete on important points. Second, the cases in this chapter do not conform as closely to the ideal of the "most similar" research design. The countries included in the analysis here differ from one another in ways that might influence their willingness and ability to share intelligence with the United States. All the European countries are wealthy and all ruled by democratic governments, whereas those in the Middle East and Central Asia are neither. It is possible that differences like these, in addition to the variables identified by relational contracting, affect decisions to share intelligence.

In addition to revealing the extent and form of contemporary intelligence-sharing arrangements, transactions cost economics provides some insight into the question of intelligence reform in the United States. Many analysts and blue-ribbon panels have suggested that the American intelligence community's top priority should be strengthening its ability to collect human intelligence rather than relying on other states to pass along this information. Daniel Byman advises that "to reduce its vulnerability to manipulation, the United States should also try to diversify its intelligence sources to ensure that it does not rely exclusively on the local ally for information."[39] Senator Saxby Chambliss (R-Ga.), a member of the Senate Select Committee on Intelligence, concluded that "the CIA had lost its focus on [human intelligence] missions and needed to put more collectors on the streets, rely less on other foreign intelligence agencies, and find ways to penetrate terrorist cells."[40] This criticism was also emphasized in the independent investigations of the terrorist attack by al Qaeda on September 11, 2001, as well as the U.S. intelligence community's incorrect conclusion that Iraq possessed weapons of mass destruction before the American invasion of the country in 2003.[41]

The U.S. intelligence community has sought to expand substantially its human intelligence capabilities directed against terrorist organizations. But there are important limits to what this will accomplish. The intelligence community has found it difficult to recruit enough people with the language skills and cultural backgrounds most useful for collecting human intelligence on Islamic terrorism. The fact that the large majority of the members and supporters of Islamic terrorist groups are located outside the United States places logistical and political limits on how far American intelligence officers can go to obtain such intelligence, as even friendly countries often object to their collecting human intelligence on their territory. Furthermore, it is not clear that the United States has tried to limit or replace in any significant way intelligence sharing with other states. Indeed, as the case studies make clear, the United States has greatly increased its sharing with the rest of the world, and especially with countries with strong incentives to renege on such sharing. The reason for this, I suggest, is that American intelligence agencies understand that there are practical limits to expanding human intelligence collection and that they can use hierarchy to better ensure that partners overseas will not refuse to supply them with such intelligence. Clearly recognizing and understanding the costs and benefits of hierarchical arrangements, compared with the proposals of intelligence reform advocates, may lead to a reevaluation of the development of a stronger American effort to collect human intelligence directly.

In this last chapter, I review the findings in the different chapters and develop a more comprehensive empirical reckoning for how well the expectations about intelligence sharing derived from relational contracting accounts for the actual patterns of cooperation. I use two methods to evaluate these expectations: comparisons of cases that are "most similar" on other variables that might influence the propensity to share intelligence, and process tracing the decisions whether to share intelligence and how to structure sharing relationships.

FINDINGS

The first expectation holds that the promise of large potential gains is a necessary condition for intelligence sharing due to monitoring problems. This expectation receives strong support from the case histories. In every case, process tracing reveals that the potential for large intelligence gains for the recipient state was an important motive for engaging in intelligence sharing. In no case considered here was it not possible to clearly identify such gains.

Comparisons of otherwise similar cases also support this expectation of relational contracting. Consider France and Germany during the early cold war. American officials concluded that both were substantial security risks. Where they differed was in the intelligence they could supply to the United States. France had little intelligence of much value. But Germany offered a great deal of useful intelligence, leading the United States to construct a hierarchical relationship in order to gain access to this intelligence while at the same time reducing the possibility of German defection. This comparison is not perfect, however, because the two countries did differ on one important variable, the costs of developing and maintaining a hierarchy. These costs were lower for Germany because the United States occupied the country and later exercised an unusual degree of control over Germany's military and security policies.

A better comparison is American intelligence sharing with South Vietnam before and after the United States' adoption of the pacification strategy. This strategy substantially increased the value that the United States attached to intelligence offered by the South Vietnamese government. But the periods before and after the switch to the pacification strategy are similar in their other potential influences on intelligence sharing, including the identity of the participants, their interests outside pacification, their relative power, and the costs of moving to a hierarchical relationship.

Another comparison of similar cases is the United States' sharing intelligence with countries in Europe and the Middle East before and after the terrorist attacks of September 11, 2001. These events quickly made obtaining intelligence on Islamic terrorism the highest priority of American foreign policy. Because some countries in Europe and the Middle East had access to much intelligence on this topic, the United States decided to deepen its intelligence-sharing relationships.

The second expectation holds that states share intelligence through anarchic institutions if they believe that their partners are unlikely to defect. The comparison of intelligence sharing with Britain and Germany best evaluates this expectation. Both countries were able to provide the United States with valuable intelligence. Whereas Germany was seen as likely to defect, Britain was viewed as a reliable ally. The outcome in this case was anarchic sharing with Britain, which is consistent with this expectation. Comparing the process-tracing evidence in these two cases also supports this expectation. American officials spent much time and energy discussing how they could structure their intelligence relationship with Germany to prevent defection, but there is little evidence that they worried a great deal about British defection or sought to construct elaborate mechanisms for ensuring British compliance. This comparison, then, supports the expectation's main claim.

Two factors do somewhat limit confidence in this conclusion. First, I analyze only one case here with the outcome of anarchic sharing, but the comparison and analysis of more cases might allow more definitive conclusions about this expectation. Second, many of the internal documents that deal directly with the guidelines for sharing intelligence between Britain and the United States remain classified. It is possible that American officials seriously considered constructing a hierarchical intelligence-sharing relationship with Britain but, for some reason, did not. But I think that this is unlikely because it would have been difficult to keep this secret for so long and because there is no evidence that American officials sought to restructure their relationship with Britain along hierarchical lines even when they may have had good reason and the power to do so, such as after the revelation of spying for the Soviet Union by senior British officials or after the Suez affair in the late 1950s.

According to the third expectation, if at least one state estimates that the other's incentives to defect are high, it will construct a hierarchical relationship to govern intelligence sharing when the benefits from sharing are thought to be greater than the costs of creating and maintaining the hierarchy plus the (now reduced) costs of defection. Much, but not all, of the evidence is consistent with this expectation. Consider the cases in which the benefits of cooperation were substantial and the likelihood of defection was high but the costs of creating and maintaining a hierarchy varied. Three comparisons satisfy these criteria at least minimally. The first compares the experience of West Germany in the 1940s and 1950s with American attempts to cooperate with Pakistan after 2001. In both cases, the United States hoped to obtain much useful intelligence from its partner but also had important reservations about the other state's reliability. These two cases differed on the third variable identified by relational contracting: the costs of creating and maintaining a hierarchical intelligence-sharing relationship. These costs were likely lower in the case of West Germany because the United States was its principal guarantor against the Soviets and because the United States played an unusually direct role in overseeing the Federal Republic's security policy. American officials would like to have had similar control over Pakistan's intelligence-sharing efforts as well. But Pakistan has resisted this control more consistently and vehemently than did West Germany during the

early cold war period, so the United States decided that direct controlling Pakistani intelligence would be too costly and difficult to be worth
the effort.

A second set of cases that conform more closely to the most similar
research designs are the United States' sharing intelligence with Pakistan compared with other countries in the Middle East, such as Jordan,
Egypt, and Morocco. These three countries were willing to allow the
United States to directly influence much of their intelligence on Islamic
terrorism. The governments of these countries also were more willing to
participate in an American-led intelligence effort than were Pakistan's
leaders. This has reduced the expense for the United States of creating
and maintaining hierarchical relationships with the three countries.

Much of the process-tracing evidence is consistent with this expectation about the conditions under which hierarchy is deemed worthwhile.
In all the cases of hierarchical intelligence sharing, there is evidence that
decision makers considered how well a hierarchy might reduce incentives
to defect and how they could balance the costs of hierarchy against this
benefit. This evidence is clearest for West Germany and South Vietnam
after 1967. In both, American decision makers insisted that they needed
to have direct control over their partner's intelligence efforts in order
to forestall defection, and they used terminology analogous to hierarchy
to describe the type of relationship they preferred. They employed the
specific mechanisms for establishing hierarchy discussed in chapter 1,
including seconding personnel, providing financing, and training their
partner's intelligence and security personnel.

American decision makers also discussed how the costs of hierarchy
could be best balanced against its benefits, for example, how much access
the United States needed to the West German intelligence service's personnel records and whether it needed to create policies concerning the
involvement of American personnel in the detention and interrogation
of prisoners in South Vietnam. Both these measures imposed unwanted
constraints on the activities of the other countries' intelligence services,
and the Americans tried to make sure that the difficulties they created
were worthwhile.

Because I did not have access to internal documents, I had difficulty
determining whether the debates about intelligence sharing with Colombia, Morocco, Jordan, and Egypt—all relationships characterized by
hierarchy—were consistent with this expectation. There does seem to be

considerable evidence, though, that the United States saw hierarchy as an effective way to prevent defection in these cases. Especially important here is the fact that American personnel were assigned to participate directly in some of the most sensitive intelligence collection activities conducted by the subordinate states, including monitoring the communications of drug traffickers in Colombia and overseeing the interrogations of suspected terrorists in the other three countries. With the partial exception of communications surveillance in Colombia, American personnel are unlikely to have had training or technical knowledge that allowed them to contribute much to the efficacy of these efforts. This indicates that their involvement was driven more by a desire to monitor rather than to contribute to these states' intelligence efforts. Finally, the type of process-tracing evidence highlighted by relational contracting also is consistent with the absence of hierarchy in the European Union and in the United States' intelligence relationship with Pakistan. Political leaders in the European Union have been unable to create a hierarchical structure to govern their intelligence sharing because, according to the concerns articulated by many governments in their public statements and in their preference for weak European Union rules, the costs to them for less decision-making freedom would not be offset by improved sharing. As discussed earlier, American officials have regularly admitted privately that they wanted to create a hierarchy in their intelligence relationship with Pakistan but that Islamabad opposed it.

This expectation about hierarchy captures a key contribution of this book to our understanding of intelligence sharing, and so it is important to show the extent to which the evidence presented here does or does not support it. The comparisons of these most similar cases do not offer ironclad support for this expectation. First, it is not clear whether they are sufficiently similar across other factors that might influence the likelihood of creating a hierarchical intelligence-sharing relationship. More problematic here is the comparison of West Germany and Pakistan, which differ in many ways: world region, regime type, level of economic development, and types of security threats. It is difficult to determine whether any of these differences shaped each country's intelligence relationship with the United States. The comparison of Pakistan with other countries in the Middle East is less problematic in this regard, since all these countries view al Qaeda as a threat to their security, share a secular orientation, are not democracies, and so on.

A second problem with drawing clear conclusions from these compari-sons is that the three key variables—the benefits of sharing, the likelihood and costs of defection, and the costs of creating and maintaining a hier-archical relationship—cannot be precisely measured, meaning that their relationships with the outcome of interest may differ from my interpreta-tions. Nonetheless, these difficulties should not mean that my argument about intelligence sharing should be rejected. None of the comparisons leads to the conclusion that the relational contracting understanding of the emergence of hierarchy is incorrect; instead, alternative interpreta-tions might conclude that in these cases, the relationships are simply are too ambiguous either to support or reject the theory. Furthermore, the fact that the other expectations described in chapter 1 are not supported by more evidence indicates that the argument of this book has captured at least some of the elements regarding the sources of hierarchical in-telligence sharing. The fact that much of the process-tracing evidence is consistent with relational contracting theory's expectations also may demonstrate that the theory has shed light on the origins of hierarchy. Finally, no other explanation discussed in detail here, such as the focus on mutual trust or neoliberal institutionalism, can account for hierarchical relationships in international politics. Even if my explanation of hierar-chy completely contradicted the evidence, relational contracting makes an important contribution by identifying hierarchy as a type of coopera-tion common in international intelligence sharing.

The final expectation states that power imbalances between dominant and subordinate states are a necessary but not sufficient condition for creating a hierarchy, that every case of hierarchy should be characterized by such a power imbalance. This is clearly true for the cases considered here. The six cases of hierarchy—West Germany in the early cold war, South Vietnam in the late 1960s and early 1970s, Colombia after 1998, and Jordan, Egypt, and Morocco after 2000—all are characterized by a dominant United States with far more material resources than its part-ners. The expectation also implies that even when the other conditions for a hierarchy are in place but the participating states are of roughly equal power, they will not be able to create such a relationship. As dis-cussed in chapter 4, the failure to strengthen intelligence sharing in the European Union is consistent with this view. Although the countries of the European Union satisfy the other conditions for forming a hierarchi-cal relationship, such as the large potential gains from more sharing and concerns about defection, they do not include a state that could shoulder a disproportionate share of the costs of hierarchy or has the resources to punish defectors. A final implication of the expectation is that hierarchy should not be formed when the dominant state does not perceive substantial gains from improved intelligence sharing. The cases of France in the cold war and South Vietnam before 1968 bear this out. In both situations, the United States had the material resources to create a hierarchy but declined to do so because it saw few benefits from greater sharing with these countries.

IMPLICATIONS FOR THE STUDY OF INTELLIGENCE

This book's general approach is that intelligence sharing is a form of cooperation that can be analyzed and understood using the basic tools of social science, including the systematic description of patterns of behavior, the development of hypothesized causes of this behavior, and a clearly articulated and methodical research design that allows for the rigorous collection of evidence. To the extent that this approach has merit, it has implications for the study of intelligence and for the relevance of this work to decision makers and the evaluation of intelligence policies.

The study of intelligence might be considered an important part of the broader study of international relations and foreign policy, but Amy Zegart has shown that this is not the case. That is, intelligence does not fit neatly into existing fields of inquiry, and the secrecy of many intelligence agencies makes it difficult for outsiders to obtain reliable information about their activities.[1] The many fine works on intelligence cited throughout this book should demonstrate that serious study of intelligence is possible and rewarding. It is also increasingly important for an accurate understanding of many of the security challenges that are likely to dominate world politics for the foreseeable future. Terrorism is a good example. As discussed in chapter 5, access to accurate intelligence, more than a preponderance of resources such as military power, is often decisive in counterterrorism campaigns.

The understanding of the benefits and limits of intelligence for public policy could be further strengthened if more analysis were closely tied to existing explanatory frameworks in the social sciences. This book has viewed intelligence sharing through the lens of theories of relational contracting that have been used to understand a range of social phenomena, from the organization of firms to the formation and dissolution of empires. Others have drawn on psychological theories to explain barriers to effective intelligence analysis and on organizational cultures and domestic politics to better understand intelligence failures and the fate of intelligence reform efforts.[2] How states collect (or fail to collect) intelligence, analyze this intelligence (poorly or well), and use the results to inform debates and decisions need to be better understood. Some scholars who study intelligence have been trained as historians or policy analysts rather than social scientists. Their work could benefit from a more sustained interaction with the theories and empirical research practices that are commonly employed in the social sciences. I would argue that more attention to well-developed theory could improve the study of intelligence in two ways.

First, theories drawn from other areas of social life may lead to unexpected questions and answers. For example, the theory of relational contracting explains how states can structure their relationships through hierarchy to better realize mutual gains from cooperation. This outcome of hierarchy is not uncommon in international intelligence sharing, as my case studies make clear. Yet despite the empirical importance of hierarchy, it has received no systematic attention in the existing research on intelligence sharing. A second reason for taking theory more seriously is that, as has been frequently observed, it is difficult to make any sort of generalization without theory. In other words, the analysis and conclusions of those who reject theory are in fact influenced by an implicit theory or theories of action. But the fact that these theories are not clearly articulated makes it more difficult to challenge their precepts.

To be clear, I am not advocating that theory should play a dominant role in thinking about intelligence. Theory must be disciplined and evaluated through empirical investigation. Here there may be important gains from incorporating some well-developed ideas from the social sciences about how to evaluate propositions with rigorous research designs. Such research designs not only allow the careful evaluation of theoretical propositions but also can have important practical consequences and improve the policy relevance of studies of intelligence. To take an example from this book, practitioners of intelligence regularly explain intelligence sharing as a product of states' mutual trust. Mutual trust certainly facilitates intelligence sharing, but it is not a necessary condition for sharing. States that do not place a high degree of trust in each other can, under the right conditions, still share intelligence. Many of the cases presented earlier support this proposition. Although the commonly accepted idea that trust drives cooperation in this area turns out to be an important part of the story, it is not the whole story. Rather, the options open to decision makers seeking to share intelligence differ from those prescribed by the conventional wisdom on the topic.

Policy Implications

Relational contracting can help explain why the United States has regularly developed close intelligence-sharing relationships with other governments guilty of widespread human rights abuses. Of the cases analyzed in this book, West Germany, South Vietnam, Colombia, Egypt, Jordan, and Morocco fall into this category. The West German intelligence service employed people with close links to the Nazi regime; South Vietnam repressed the political rights of its citizens and regularly used violence to prevent dissent; Colombian authorities encouraged the development of militias that undertook extrajudicial killings against its opponents; and the governments of Egypt, Jordan, and Morocco imprison and torture opponents of their rule. The complete list of countries with whom the United States has shared intelligence and that have poor human rights records is even longer than this. They include Iran under the rule of the shah from the 1950s to 1978, military regimes in Central and South America during the 1970s and early 1980s, China since the late 1970s, Saudi Arabia, Saddam Hussein's Iraq in the mid-1980s, and countries in Central Asia such as Uzbekistan after the United States' invasion of Afghanistan in 2001.[3]

Because American leaders regularly claim that the promotion of human rights is an important foreign policy priority, why have they not distanced themselves from such countries? More specifically, why have they regularly forged close, hierarchical relationships with these countries' intelligence agencies, often the very agencies responsible for much of the repression? One answer is that talk of promoting human rights is merely talk and that American decision makers are quick to forget their human rights promises when these conflict with pressing strategic or military challenges. Even if foreign policy decision makers do not attach much importance to human rights, some of their constituents and allies do and criticize their leaders for ignoring them.[4]

President George W. Bush's administration was condemned by members of Congress and countries in Europe for its overly close intelligence collaboration with governments in the Middle East and South Asia that abuse human rights. Earlier American administrations were similarly criticized for sharing intelligence with the shah's Iran, Saddam Hussein's Iraq, and other countries. Revelations about such intelligence sharing can undermine the United States' reputation. For example, evidence that the United States collaborated closely with the Iranian shah's much-feared intelligence service contributed to the deterioration of relations with the revolutionary government that overthrew his regime.

Even for leaders who reject the intrinsic importance of human rights, such intelligence sharing has a price. Relational contracting helps show why the United States has frequently maintained very close intelligence-sharing relationships with countries with poor human rights records. On the one hand, these countries have intelligence that is valuable to the United States, giving it a reason to exchange diplomatic support, military aid, or economic assistance for this intelligence. On the other hand, these governments are, from the perspective of the United States, quite likely to defect from their promises to share intelligence. Many, such as South Vietnam or Colombia, have corrupt or poorly trained security personnel that the United States cannot trust to handle intelligence securely. Others, such as Pakistan, also have foreign policy or domestic political interests that conflict with the goal of cooperating with the United States. Still other states may oppose the United States precisely because of their poor history of protecting human rights. For example, President Jimmy Carter's administration pressed the shah of Iran to improve his government's respect for human rights. But the shah complained, as he saw it as weakening his authority over Iranian society and indirectly aiding those who sought to overthrow his regime.

Relational contracting holds that in situations like these, which offer substantial gains from intelligence sharing and in which the likelihood of defection is high, states can overcome their concerns about defection by introducing hierarchy into their intelligence-sharing relationship. Hierarchy means that the dominant country, here the United States, is closely involved in many aspects of the subordinate state's intelligence activities. These activities may include abuses of human rights. In some cases, the United States tries to reduce such abuses. In South Vietnam, for example, American officials did press for the more humane treatment of detainees held by government forces, arguing that this was more likely to generate useful intelligence while also reducing criticism of the South Vietnamese regime by both its own and U.S. citizens.

Just as often, though, the subordinate state seeks to continue its abuse of human rights but tries to hide these activities from its American overseers. Colombia is a good example. Even though the Colombian government has welcomed American military and intelligence assistance for its forces since 2000, it also has secretly encouraged the development of nonofficial militias. These militias frequently abuse human rights, including killings and kidnappings. The United States then was criticized for cooperating with a government that encouraged such abuses, and many people wondered how the United States could have become so closely involved in training and supporting government agencies that, at least indirectly, oversaw the activities of these militias. The answer offered by relational contracting is that the United States faced strong incentives to supervise and control Colombia's intelligence activities but that these controls were not sufficient to prevent the state from abusing its citizens' rights.

Relational contracting also offers new perspectives on the issue of intelligence reform in the United States. American intelligence agencies have been strongly criticized for not sharing intelligence with one another. This failure to share prevented them from stopping the terrorist attacks of September 11, 2001. Subsequent investigations revealed that different intelligence agencies had important information about elements of this terrorist plot but failed to "connect the dots" in a way that would have allowed them to thwart the attack. The federal government has since attached great importance to improving all aspects of intelligence collection and analysis.[5]

Three remedies have been offered to correct these failings: organizational change, additional human intelligence sources and less reliance on other countries for human intelligence, and more emphasis on sharing intelligence among U.S. government agencies concerned with national security policy. The application of relational contracting to intelligence sharing brings to bear new perspectives and ideas about the second and third proposal.[6]

Many argue that the U.S. intelligence community needs to improve its ability to gather human intelligence from spies, defectors, and/or refugees. During the cold war with the Soviet Union, American intelligence agencies developed extensive technical means of collecting intelligence, by focusing much of their effort on networks of sophisticated and expensive satellites and communication interception capabilities. Current challenges can also use such technical collection means, of course, but reliable human intelligence is especially important. Terrorism is a good example. As discussed in chapter 5, terrorist groups rely on their ability to hide their activities, plans, and communications from government authorities. They seek to avoid detection by, for example, avoiding communication devices that might be monitored by intelligence agencies and by locating their activities in remote areas or hiding among urban populations. Human intelligence provided by captured or erstwhile terrorists is an effective way to overcome this secrecy to obtain the information needed to disrupt a terrorist organization.

Human intelligence can also be very useful against another major threat to international security, the proliferation of weapons of mass destruction. Like terrorists, those states seeking these weapons have become adept at masking their activities to avoid detection by satellites and other technical means.[7] Even when such technical intelligence is available, it cannot provide much information about the states' ultimate intentions. Some states seek to develop a full range of weapons of mass destruction, whereas the only intention of others is to explore these weapons' technologies or to enable them to develop the weapons if or when a foe does so.[8] Weapons development in some countries, such as Iran, is closely protected from public scrutiny and may be influenced by political conflicts among government leaders and bureaucracies that are difficult for outsiders to comprehend. Technical intelligence cannot distinguish these different motives and complex internal political dynamics. Nonetheless, knowledge of such motives and dynamics is very important to crafting a counterproliferation strategy.

Human intelligence, in contrast, can obtain information about the intentions and strategies of political, scientific, and military leaders overseeing weapons development. But obtaining human intelligence on such targets is very difficult. Aware of the intense interest of foreign intelligence agencies in their weapons development, such targets implement security measures and carefully screen personnel to ensure secrecy. An additional difficulty that the United States in particular faces is that few of its intelligence personnel have the requisite language skills or cultural knowledge to circulate unnoticed among the targets of greatest intelligence interest in East Asia, the Middle East, and South Asia. Instead, the United States relies on allied intelligence services to share their human intelligence. These countries often do have intelligence personnel with the skills needed to collect such intelligence, and their proximity to the target means that they also have access to individuals, such as refugees or business travelers, who may be able to share such intelligence. The difficulty is that these governments may demand a high price in exchange for sharing this intelligence with the United States, or they may agree to share intelligence and subsequently renege on this promise. Concerns about such bargaining and enforcement problems have led many people to recommend that the United States minimize its reliance on partners by substantially expanding its own capacity to collect human intelligence.

Implementing this recommendation is costly and time-consuming and may not produce the desired outcomes. The financial cost of expanding human intelligence capabilities would be small for the United States, which spends a great deal of money on technical intelligence collection. It would exact a high price, though, to secure the attention of senior political and intelligence leaders, who would need to spend scarce time and energy to overseeing this expansion.

Moreover, there is no guarantee that attaching a higher priority to human intelligence would produce adequate results. Besides the difficulty of recruiting and training staff with the appropriate skills, high-quality human sources are very difficult to find. The relational contracting account of intelligence sharing suggests that under the right conditions, hierarchy is another option that needs to be considered in addition to the current dependence on unreliable partners for intelligence or the dramatic expansion of the United States' human intelligence capabilities. As it did in West Germany and South Vietnam, hierarchical intelligence-sharing relationships allow the United States to exploit the more effective human intelligence capabilities of a subordinate state while also closely monitoring it for defection. This does not mean that strengthening human intelligence efforts is undesirable. The United States will always need to be able to collect human intelligence in order to ascertain the accuracy of intelligence shared by other states and in situations in which no other state is willing or able to share its intelligence. What it does mean, though, is that the option of a dramatic expansion of human intelligence is based on an incomplete understanding of how the United States can alleviate its concerns about defection and that therefore the intelligence community may have other options for more effective and secure sharing with other countries through hierarchy that need to be considered in this policy debate.

Finally, future research could push relational contracting to explore intelligence sharing among units of the same national government. There have been many calls to improve intelligence sharing in the U.S. government. Advocates of greater sharing observe that often different government agencies independently collect much useful intelligence on a target of interest but that it is never pulled together or analyzed as a whole. This has been an important issue of intelligence reform since the terrorist attacks of September 11, 2001, before which various U.S. law enforcement and intelligence agencies had collected important clues to the impending attack. But it is a long-standing problem. Writing almost five decades ago, Roberta Wohlstetter identified the same problem in the United States' actions before the attack on Pearl Harbor in 1941.[9]

Relational contracting may be able to add to our understanding of why internal intelligence sharing has not been fully exploited and to suggest possible responses. At first glance, this claim is surprising because relational contracting identifies hierarchy as the solution to many of the problems of intelligence sharing. U.S. intelligence agencies are, of course, already organized in a formal hierarchy. The president or the director of national intelligence already has the authority to require agencies to take certain actions, such as sharing intelligence with one another, and to monitor their compliance. This formal hierarchy does not apply to the international realm, in which no state has a right to command another and in which hierarchy in intelligence sharing is instead negotiated. Any understanding of domestic intelligence sharing would need to consider the power and authority of government leaders to order the state's other arms to cooperate. But any assumption that these leaders can automatically use this authority to effect changes may be overstated.

The U.S. intelligence community's long history of suboptimal sharing and cooperation is matched by its long history of resisting demands from the White House, Congress, and others that it improve its sharing practices. In this sense, the intelligence community does resemble the anarchic state of international politics, as the individual agencies appear to have some room to make autonomous decisions about the terms under which they will cooperate with one another.[10] This means that those who oversee the intelligence community may have only a limited ability to *command* greater sharing. They may, however, be able to draw on some of the incentives that states have used to monitor and influence the sharing of their partners. These include offering financial inducements, borrowing personnel, and providing training. The new head of the intelligence community, the Office of the Director of National Intelligence (ODNI), does not completely control the budgets of all the intelligence agencies. But this office could use the limited budgetary authority it does have to reward agencies that share with others and to punish those that do not. Furthermore, while the ODNI does not directly control the entire intelligence budget, the office does have some authority to review this spending. This budgetary review authority could help encourage intelligence sharing by estimating the extent to which intelligence agencies prioritize and share with others. Borrowing personnel and training also could serve as an important spur to greater sharing, although this is unlikely to produce immediate results. Recent requirements that intelligence personnel must serve outside their home agencies if they wish to be promoted to senior levels may encourage greater mutual trust among different agencies in the same way that multispeed cooperation in the European Union has done so. The ODNI does have substantial influence over training of intelligence personnel, shaping through socialization how future managers will perceive the advantages and costs of sharing with their counterparts in other agencies.

1. Understanding Intelligence Sharing

1. The most thorough account of this incident is Bob Drogin, *Curveball: Spies, Lies, and the Con Man Who Caused a War* (New York: Random House, 2007).

2. See, especially, Daniel Byman, *The Five Front War: The Better Way to Fight Global Jihad* (New York: Wiley, 2008), 83–92; National Commission on Terrorist Attacks upon the United States, *Final Report of the National Commission on Terrorist Attacks on the United States* (Washington, D.C.: Government Printing Office, 2004); and Ahmed Rashid, *Descent into Chaos: The United States and the Failure of Nation Building in Pakistan, Afghanistan, and Central Asia* (New York: Viking, 2008).

3. Michael Warner considers different definitions of intelligence in "Wanted: A Definition of 'Intelligence,'" *Studies in Intelligence* 46, no. 3 (2002): 15–22. The definition of intelligence used here excludes activities often carried out by national governments' intelligence agencies, such as covert action, the use of paramilitary forces, and propaganda, and instead focuses on these organizations' efforts to gather, secure, and place policy-relevant information in the proper context.

4. Charles Lipson, "International Cooperation in Economic and Security Affairs," *World Politics* 37, no. 1 (1984): 1–23.

5. Bradley F. Smith, *Sharing Secrets with Stalin: How the Allies Traded Intelligence, 1941–45* (Lawrence: University Press of Kansas, 1996).

6. James Fearon, "Bargaining, Enforcement, and International Cooperation," *International Organization* 52, no. 2 (1998): 269–306; Walter Mattli, *The Logic of Regional Integration* (Cambridge: Cambridge University Press, 1999).

7. Lloyd Gruber, *Ruling the World* (Princeton, N.J.: Princeton University Press, 2000); Stephen D. Krasner, "Global Communications and National Power: Life on the Pareto Frontier," *World Politics* 43, no. 3 (1991): 336–66; Thomas Oatley and Robert Nabors, "Redistributive Cooperation: Market Failures and Wealth Transfers in the Creation of the Basel Accord," *International Organization* 52 (1998): 35–54.

8. There is a large literature on enforcement, and three of the most important works are Robert O. Keohane, *After Hegemony* (Princeton, N.J.: Princeton University Press, 1984); Kenneth Oye, ed., *Cooperation Under Anarchy* (Princeton, N.J.: Princeton University Press, 1985); and Arthur Stein, *Why Nations Cooperate* (Ithaca, N.Y.: Cornell University Press, 1990).

9. One of the first to make this point was Roger Hilsman Jr., "Intelligence and Policy-Making in Foreign Affairs," *World Politics* 7 (1952): 1–45.

10. Michael Herman, *Intelligence Power in Peace and War* (Cambridge: Cambridge University Press, 1996), 69–70; see also 40.

11. There is a large literature on intelligence sharing. Important works include Jeffrey T. Richelson, "The Calculus of Intelligence Cooperation," *International Journal of Intelligence and Counterintelligence* 4, no. 3 (1990): 307–23; and H. Bradford Westerfield, "America and the World of Intelligence Liaison," *Intelligence and National Security* 11, no. 3 (1996): 523–60. Other important works include Richard J. Aldrich, "Dangerous Liaisons: Post–September 11 Intelligence Alliances," *Harvard International Review*, fall 2002, 50–54; Chris Clough, "Quid Pro Quo: The Challenges of International Strategic Intelligence Cooperation," *International Journal of Intelligence and Counterintelligence* 17 (2004): 601–13; Jason D. Ellis and Geoffrey D. Kiefer, *Combating Proliferation: Strategic Intelligence and Security Policy* (Baltimore: Johns Hopkins University Press, 2007); Stephen Lander, "International Intelligence Cooperation: An Inside Perspective," *Cambridge Review of International Affairs* 17, no. 3 (2004): 481–93; Stéphane Lefebvre, "The Difficulties and Dilemmas of International Intelligence Cooperation," *International Journal of Intelligence and Counterintelligence* 16 (2003): 527–42; Michael Warner, "Intelligence Transformation and Intelligence Liaison," *SAIS Review* 24, no. 1 (2004): 77–89; Jennifer Sims, "Foreign Intelligence Liaison: Devils, Deals, and Details," *International Journal of Intelligence and Counterintelligence* 19, no. 2 (2006): 195–217; and James J. Wirtz, "Constraints on Intelligence Collaboration: The Domestic Dimension," *International Journal of Intelligence and Counterintelligence* 6, no. 1 (1993): 85–99.

12. Lefebvre, "Difficulties and Dilemmas of International Intelligence Cooperation," 528–29; Clough, "Quid Pro Quo," 603; Derek Reveron, "Old

Allies, New Friends: Intelligence-Sharing in the War on Terror," *Orbis* 50, no. 3 (2006): 456.

13. In political sociology, see James S. Coleman, *Foundations of Social Theory* (Cambridge, Mass.: Belknap Press of Harvard University Press, 1990); and Russell Hardin, *Trust and Trustworthiness* (New York: Russell Sage, 2002). The groundbreaking work in social psychology is Charles Hovland, Irving Janis, and H. Kelley, *Persuasion and Communication* (New Haven, Conn.: Yale University Press, 1953). For social constructivism, see Alexander Wendt, *Social Theory of International Politics* (Cambridge: Cambridge University Press, 1999), 359. Game theory typically does not use the term *trust,* but work on "cheap talk" analyzes when a receiver will believe information communicated by a sender. The seminal paper is Vincent P. Crawford and Joel Sobel, "Strategic Information Transmission," *Econometrica* 50 (1982): 1431–51.

14. Key works include Robert Axelrod and Robert O. Keohane, "Achieving Cooperation Under Anarchy: Strategies and Institutions," *World Politics* 38, no. 1 (1985): 226–54; Fearon, "Bargaining, Enforcement, and International Cooperation"; Charles Glaser, "Realists as Optimists: Cooperation as Self-Help," *International Security* 19, no. 1 (1995): 50–93; Keohane, *After Hegemony;* Stephen Krasner, ed., *International Regimes* (Ithaca, N.Y.: Cornell University Press, 1983); Charles Lipson, Duncan Snidal, and Barbara Koromenos, eds., "The Rational Design of International Institutions," special issue of *International Organization* 55, no. 4 (2001); Lisa Martin, *Coercive Cooperation* (Princeton, N.J.: Princeton University Press, 1992); and Oye, *Cooperation Under Anarchy.*

15. Page Fortna, *Peace Time* (Cambridge: Cambridge University Press, 2004).

16. The most influential statement of the role of information in international organizations is Keohane, *After Hegemony.*

17. An analysis of intelligence sharing in the North Atlantic Treaty Organization (NATO) is Paul B. Stares, *Command Performance: The Neglected Dimension of European Security* (Washington, D.C.: Brookings Institution, 1990). Timothy Crawford discusses intelligence sharing through the United Nations in "Why Ever Not Never? Intelligence Cooperation in United Nations Security Affairs" (paper prepared for the annual conference of the Canadian Association for Security and Intelligence Studies, Ottawa, September 26–28, 2002).

18. George W. Downs and Michael A. Jones, "Reputation, Compliance, and International Law," *Journal of Legal Studies* 31 (2002): 95–114.

19. These ideas were developed and applied to the organization of firms by Ronald H. Coase, "The Nature of the Firm," *Economica* 4 (1937): 386–405, and "The Problem of Social Cost," *Journal of Law and Economics* 3 (1960): 1–44; and Oliver Williamson, *Markets and Hierarchies: Analysis and Antitrust Implications* (New York: Free Press, 1975), and *The Economic Implications of Capitalism: Firms, Markets, and Relational Contracting* (New York: Free Press, 1985). Good

overviews that provide more detailed discussions than the short summary in this paragraph include Jeffrey T. Macher and Barak D. Richman, "Transaction Cost Economics: An Assessment of Empirical Research in the Social Sciences," *Business and Politics* 10, no. 1 (2008); and Gary Miller, *Managerial Dilemmas: The Political Economy of Hierarchy* (Cambridge: Cambridge University Press, 1992).

20. Important works that have applied relational contracting to international politics include David A. Lake, "Anarchy, Hierarchy, and the Variety of International Institutions," *International Organization* 50 (1996): 1–33; *Entangling Relations: American Foreign Policy in Its Century* (Princeton, N.J.: Princeton University Press, 1999); and "Escape from the State-of-Nature: Authority and Hierarchy in World Politics," *International Security* 32, no. 1 (2007): 47–79; Katja Weber, "Hierarchy Amidst Anarchy: A Transaction Costs Approach to International Security Cooperation," *International Studies Quarterly* 41 (1997): 321–40; and Jeffrey A. Freiden, "International Investment and Colonial Control: A New Interpretation," *International Organization* 48 (1994): 559–93.

21. See, especially, Lake, *Entangling Relations*.

22. Miller defines a hierarchy as "the asymmetric and incompletely defined authority of one actor to direct the activities of another within certain bounds" (*Managerial Dilemmas*, 16).

23. Lake, "Escape from the State-of-Nature."

24. Williamson, *Markets and Hierarchies*, 20.

25. Mattli, *Logic of Regional Integration*.

26. Works that imply that more powerful states, especially the United States, use their greater resources to insist on hierarchical arrangement in the deployment, basing, and use of military force include Andrew Bacevich, *The New American Militarism* (New York: Oxford University Press, 2005); and Chalmers Johnson, *The Sorrows of Empire: Militarism, Secrecy, and the End of the Republic* (New York: Metropolitan Books, 2006). See also Robert Jervis, "The Compulsive Empire," *Foreign Policy*, July–August 2003, 83–87.

27. See the discussion in Lake, "Escape from the State-of-Nature."

28. Krasner, "Global Communications and National Power."

29. Important recent exceptions include Uri-Bar Joseph and Rose McDermott, "Change the Analyst, Not the System: A Different Approach to Intelligence Reform," *Foreign Policy Analysis* 4, no. 2 (2008): 127–45; Thomas H. Hammond, "Why Is the Intelligence Community So Difficult to Redesign? Smart Practices, Conflicting Goals, and the Creation of Purpose-Built Organizations," *Governance* 20, no. 3 (2007): 401–22; and Amy Zegart, *Spying Blind: The CIA, the FBI, and the Origins of 9/11* (Princeton, N.J.: Princeton University Press, 2007).

30. Influential histories include Christopher Andrew, "The Making of the Anglo-American SIGINT Alliance," in *In the Name of Intelligence: Essays in Honor of Walter Pforzheimer*, ed. Hayden B. Peake and Samuel Halpern (Washington, D.C.: NIBC Press, 1994), 95–109; Richard J. Aldrich, *The Hidden Hand: Britain, America, and Cold War Secret Intelligence* (New York: Overlook Press, 2002); Andrew Cockburn and Leslie Cockburn, *Dangerous Liaison: The Inside Story of the U.S.–Israeli Covert Relationship* (New York: HarperCollins, 1991); Martin S. Alexander, ed., "Special Issue on Knowing Your Friends: Intelligence Inside Alliances from 1914 to the Cold War," *Intelligence and National Security* 13, no. 1 (1998); Jay Jakub, *Spies and Saboteurs: Anglo-American Collaboration and Rivalry in Human Intelligence Collection and Special Operations, 1940–45* (London: Macmillan, 1998); Yossi Melmanand and Dan Raviv, *Friends in Deed: Inside the U.S.–Israel Alliance* (New York: Hyperion, 1994); Jeffrey T. Richelson and Desmond Ball, *The Ties That Bind: Intelligence Cooperation Between the UKUSA Countries—The United Kingdom, the United States of America, Canada, Australia and New Zealand*, 2d ed. (Boston: Unwin Hyman, 1990); Bradley F. Smith, *The ULTRA-MAGIC Deals and the Most Secret Special Relationship, 1940–1946* (Novato, Calif.: Presidio Press, 1993), and *Sharing Secrets with Stalin;* and Rolf Tamnes, *The United States and the Cold War in the High North* (Albershot: Dartmouth, 1991).

31. This selection effect is true for studies of intelligence more generally as well. See John Ferris, "Coming in from the Cold War: The Historiography of American Intelligence, 1945–1990," *Diplomatic History* 19, no. 1 (1995): 90.

32. John Gerring, *Case Study Research: Principles and Practices* (Cambridge: Cambridge University Press, 2006), 131–39; Arend Lijphart, "The Comparable Cases Strategy in Comparative Research," *Comparative Political Studies* 8 (1975): 158–77; Adam Przeworski and Henry Tuene, *The Logic of Comparative Social Inquiry* (New York: Wiley, 1970); Theda Skocpol and Margaret Somers, "The Use of Comparative History in Macrosocial Inquiry," *Comparative Studies in Society and History* 22, no. 2 (1984): 147–97.

33. Alexander George and Timothy McKeown, "Case Studies and Theories of Organizational Decision Making," *Advances in Information Processing in Organizations* 2 (1985): 21–58; Alexander George and Andrew Bennett, *Case Studies and Theory Development* (Cambridge, Mass.: MIT Press, 2005).

34. For similar discussions of relationships between social scientific analysis and foreign policy analysis, see Alexander George, *Bridging the Gap: Theory and Practice in Foreign Policy* (Washington, D.C.: U.S. Institute of Peace, 1993); and Joseph Lepgold and Miroslav Nincic, *Beyond the Ivory Tower: International Relations Theory and the Issue of Policy Relevance* (New York: Columbia University Press, 2002). For discussions in the context of intelligence, see Loch K. Johnson,

"Bricks and Mortar for a Theory of Intelligence," *Comparative Strategy* 22, no. 1 (2003): 1–28; and Gregory F. Treverton, Seth G. Jones, Steven Boraz, and Philip Lipscy, *Toward a Theory of Intelligence: Workshop Report* (Santa Monica, Calif.: RAND Corporation, 2006).

2. TRANSATLANTIC INTELLIGENCE SHARING DURING THE COLD WAR

1. This investigation was by the Nazi War Crimes and Japanese Imperial Government Records Interagency Working Group. The group's preliminary report was written by Richard Breitman, Norman Goda, Timothy Naftali, and Robert Wolfe, *U.S. Intelligence and the Nazis* (Washington, D.C.: National Archive Trust Fund Board, 2004). Some of the most important of these declassified documents are now available online. See Tamara Feinstein, ed., *The CIA and Nazi War Criminals: National Security Archive Electronic Briefing Book No. 146*, available at http://www.gwu.edu/~nsarchiv/NSAEBB/NSAEBB 146/#2 (accessed July 15, 2006). Since not all the documents cited here are included in this online collection, I have cited their original National Archives location.

2. John Lewis Gaddis, *Strategies of Containment: A Critical Appraisal of Postwar American National Security Policy* (New York: Oxford University Press, 1982); Melvyn P. Leffler, "The American Conception of National Security and the Beginnings of the Cold War, 1945–48," *American Historical Review* 89 (1984): 357–58; James McCallister, *No Exit: America and the German Problem, 1943–1954* (Ithaca, N.Y.: Cornell University Press, 2002); R. Harrison Wagner, "What Was Bipolarity?" *International Organization* 47 (1993): 88.

3. Gar Alperovitz, *Atomic Diplomacy: Hiroshima and Potsdam* (New York: Simon and Schuster, 1965); Walter LeFeber, *America, Russia, and the Cold War, 1945–1966* (New York: Wiley, 1966); William Appleman Williams, *The Tragedy of American Diplomacy* (New York: Dell, 1972).

4. John Lewis Gaddis, *We Now Know: Rethinking Cold War History* (New York: Oxford University Press, 1997); Arnold A. Offner, *Another Such Victory: President Truman and the Cold War, 1945–1953* (Stanford, Calif.: Stanford University Press, 2002). Gaddis and Offner also emphasize how the personal experiences and biases of Truman and Soviet leader Josef Stalin, as well as their countries' political ideologies, shaped their foreign policy choices.

5. Richard J. Aldrich, *The Hidden Hand: Britain, America, and Cold War Secret Intelligence* (New York: Overlook Press, 2002), 76.

6. Matthew M. Aid, "The National Security Agency and the Cold War," in *Secrets of Signals Intelligence During the Cold War and Beyond*, ed. Matthew M. Aid and Cees Wiebes (London: Frank Cass, 2002), 28–30.

7. Richard J. Aldrich, "GCHQ and Sigint in the Early Cold War," in *Secrets of Signals Intelligence During the Cold War and Beyond,* ed. Aid and Wiebes, 77–78.

8. Richard J. Aldrich, "British Intelligence and the Anglo-American 'Special Relationship' During the Cold War," *Review of International Studies* 24 (1998): 344.

9. Bradley F. Smith, *The Ultra-Magic Deals and the Most Secret Special Relationship 1940–1946* (Novato, Calif.: Presidio Press, 1993), 224–25.

10. James Bamford, *Body of Secrets* (New York: Doubleday, 2001), 403.

11. Aldrich, *Hidden Hand,* 77.

12. Quoted in Aldrich, "GCHQ and Sigint in the Early Cold War," 84–85 (italics in original).

13. Quoted in Robert Hathaway, *Great Britain and the United States: Special Relations Since World War II* (Boston: Twayne, 1990), 12.

14. See Roosevelt's comments in William D. Hassett, *Off the Record with FDR* (New Brunswick, N.J.: Rutgers University Press, 1958), 220.

15. For Roosevelt's comments and correspondence on this point, see "The Acting Secretary of State (Stettinius) to the Ambassador in the United Kingdom (Winant)," February 26, 1944, in Department of State, *Foreign Relations of the United States, 1944* (Washington, D.C.: Government Printing Office, 1972), 1:184 (hereafter cited as *FRUS*); and "Second Plenary Meeting: Bohlen Minutes," February 5, 1945, in *FRUS 1945: The Conferences at Malta and Yalta* (Washington, D.C.: Government Printing Office, 1955), 617.

16. Marc Trachtenberg, *A Constructed Peace* (Princeton, N.J.: Princeton University Press, 1999), 66.

17. Ibid., 69–72.

18. The quotation from Bevin and Marshall's response are from "The Chargé in London (Gallman) to the Secretary of State," in *FRUS 1948* (Washington, D.C.: Government Printing Office, 1976), 3:1–2.

19. The official summary of the results of the Pentagon talks agreement is "Minutes of the Fifth Meeting of the United States–United Kingdom–Canada Security Conversations, Held at Washington, March 31, 1948," in *FRUS 1948,* 3:72–75.

20. Central Intelligence Agency, "Political and Economic Changes in Western Europe Since the Last Conference of Foreign Ministers," ORE 58–49, June 1, 1949, in *CIA Research Reports: Europe, 1945–1976* (Frederick. Md.: University Publications of America, 1982), reel 4, p. 4.

21. Central Intelligence Agency, "United Kingdom," SR-25, December 7, 1949, in *CIA Research Reports,* reel 4, p. 23.

22. See, for example, Hoyt S. Vanderburg, Director of Central Intelligence, "Memorandum for the President," February 15, 1947, in *CIA Research Reports,* reel 4.

23. Aldrich, "GCHQ and Sigint in the Early Cold War."

24. Aldrich, "British Intelligence and the Anglo-American 'Special Relationship,'" 345.

25. The most comprehensive accounts of the information passed to the Soviet Union are John Earl Haynes and Harvey Klehr, *Venona: Decoding Soviet Espionage in America* (New Haven, Conn.: Yale University Press, 1999); Verne W. Newton, *The Cambridge Spies: The Untold Story of McLean, Philby, and Burgess in America* (New York: Madison Books, 1991); and Nigel West and Oleg Tsarev, *The Crown Jewels: The British Secrets at the Heart of the KGB Archives* (New Haven, Conn.: Yale University Press, 1999).

26. Smith, *Ultra-Magic Deals*, 203.

27. Quotations from "Collaboration with the British in the Communication Intelligence Field, Continuation and Extension of," "Memorandum for the President," and "Memorandum for the Secretary of State, the Secretary of War, and the Secretary of the Navy," September 12, 1945, file 1, box 10, naval aide files, Harry S. Truman Library, Independence, Mo. See also Christopher Andrew, "The Making of the Anglo-American SIGINT Alliance, 1940–1948," in *The Intelligence Revolution and Modern Warfare*, ed. James E. Dillard and Walter T. Hitchcock (Chicago: Imprint, 1996), 93–95; and Smith, *Ultra-Magic Deals*, 211–12.

28. "The BRUSA Agreement of May 17, 1943," *Cryptologia* 21 (1997): 30–38.

29. Jeffrey T. Richelson and Desmond Ball, *The Ties That Bind: Intelligence Cooperation Between the UKUSA Countries—The United Kingdom, the United States of America, Canada, Australia and New Zealand*, 2d ed. (London: Unwin Hyman, 1990), 142–46, 257.

30. "Minutes of the 10th Meeting of the National Intelligence Authority," June 26, 1947, in *FRUS: Emergence of the Intelligence Establishment* (Washington, D.C.: Government Printing Office, 1996), 773.

31. Cord Meyer, *Facing Reality* (Lanham, Md.: University Press of America, 1980), 165–66.

32. Richelson and Ball, *Ties That Bind*, 257.

33. Aldrich, "British Intelligence and the Anglo-American 'Special Relationship,'" 342; S. J. Hamrick, *Deceiving the Deceivers* (New Haven, Conn.: Yale University Press, 2004).

34. Quoted in Daniel Yergin, *Shattered Peace: The Origins of the Cold War and the National Security State* (Boston: Houghton Mifflin, 1977), 154.

35. John Ranelagh, *The Agency: The Rise and Decline of the CIA* (New York: Simon and Schuster, 1986), 147.

36. Good accounts of the Suez conflict are David Carlton, *Britain and the Suez Crisis* (Oxford: Blackwell, 1988); Keith Kyle, *Suez* (New York: St. Martin's

Press, 1991); and William Roger Louis and Roger Owen, eds., *Suez 1956* (Oxford: Clarendon Press, 1989).

37. For details, see Scott Lucas and Alistair Morey, "The Hidden Alliance: The CIA and MI6 Before and After Suez," *Intelligence and National Security* 15 (2000): 111.

38. Newton, *Cambridge Spies*, 148–51.

39. Roger Faligot, "France, Sigint, and the Cold War," in *Secrets of Signals Intelligence During the Cold War and Beyond*, ed. Aid and Wiebes, 184, 188.

40. Roger Faligot and Pascal Krop, *La Piscine: Les services secrets français, 1944–1984* (Paris: Éditions du Seuil, 1988), 72–74.

41. Douglas Porch, *The French Secret Services: From the Dreyfus Affair to the Gulf War* (New York: Farrar, Straus and Giroux, 1995), 278. See also Carolyn Eisenberg, *Drawing the Line: The American Decision to Divide Germany, 1944–1949* (Cambridge: Cambridge University Press, 1996).

42. For the French reaction, see "Memorandum of Conversation, Byrnes and Bidault, August 23, 1945," in *FRUS 1945: Conference on Berlin* (Washington, D.C.: Government Printing Office, 1974), 1557–64.

43. Secretary of State James Byrnes's speech is reprinted in *Documents on Germany Under Occupation*, ed. Beate Ruhm von Oppen (Oxford: Oxford University Press, 1955), 152–60.

44. William I. Hitchcock, *France Restored: Cold War Diplomacy and the Quest for Leadership in Europe, 1944–1954* (Chapel Hill: University of North Carolina Press, 1998), 78–82.

45. American officials clearly communicated to their French counterparts that they would move forward with or without French support. See, for example, "The Ambassador in France (Caffery) to the Secretary of State," June 10, 1948, in *FRUS 1948* (Washington, D.C.: Government Printing Office, 1976), 2: 327–28. See also Central Intelligence Agency, "France's German Policy," ORE 39–48, December 29, 1948, in *CIA Research Reports*, reel 1.

46. Department of War, Strategic Services Unit, "Communist Activity in Southwest France," March 1946, in *CIA Research Reports*, reel 1, p. 6. See also Thierry Wolton, *Le KGB en France* (Paris: Grasset, 1986), 31.

47. Central Intelligence Agency, "France," SR-30, March 17, 1950, in *CIA Research Reports*, reel 1, p. 18.

48. See, for example, the concerns of U.S. Ambassador Jefferson Caffery discussed in Irwin Wall, *The United States and the Making of Postwar France, 1945–1954* (Cambridge: Cambridge University Press, 1991), 67–68.

49. See, for example, "The Ambassador in the United Kingdom (Douglas) to the Secretary of State," July 4, 1947, in *FRUS 1947* (Washington, D.C.: Government Printing Office, 1968), 3:310–12.

50. Philip Williams, *Wars, Plots, and Scandals in Postwar France* (Cambridge: Cambridge University Press, 1970).

51. "Security Aspects of Possible Staff Talks with France (TAB A), Belgium, Holland and Luxembourg (TAB B)," March 26, 1948, Director of Intelligence USAF HQ files, file 2–1200–1299, box 40, RG 341, United States National Archives, Washington, D.C., in Richard J. Aldrich, *Documents in Contemporary History: Espionage, Security and Intelligence in Britain, 1945–1970* (Manchester: Manchester University Press, 1998), 145–46.

52. Wall, *United States and the Making of Postwar France*, 212–13.

53. See, for example, the consultations with the French foreign minister, which do not mention this topic: "Memorandum of Conversation by the Political Advisor for Germany (Murphy)," December 17, 1947, in *FRUS 1947* (Washington, D.C.: Government Printing Office, 1975), 2:811–13.

54. Gladwyn Jebb, *The Memoirs of Lord Gladwyn* (New York: Weybright and Talley, 1972), 215; Escott Reid, *Time of Fear and Hope: The Making of the North Atlantic Treaty, 1947–1949* (Toronto: McClelland and Stewart, 1977), 99. Jebb and Reid were, respectively, senior British and Canadian officials who participated in the secret negotiation of the North Atlantic Treaty.

55. "Minutes of the First Meeting of the United States–United Kingdom–Canada Security Conversations, Held at Washington, March 22, 1948," in *FRUS 1948*, 3:59–61.

56. Faligot, "France, Sigint, and the Cold War," 193; Porch, *French Secret Services*, 292.

57. Richelson and Ball, *Ties That Bind*, 257.

58. Aldrich, "GCHQ and Sigint in the Early Cold War," 79.

59. Thomas Powers, *The Man Who Kept the Secrets: Richard Helms and the CIA* (New York: Knopf, 1979), 38. See also Headquarters, European Command, Intelligence Division to Commanding Officer, 7821 Composite Group, "Priorities for Intelligence Collection," November 30, 1948, Records of the Central Intelligence Agency, Record Group 263, RC box no. 2, 2000/06/02, National Archives, Washington, D.C.

60. James H. Critchfield, *Partners at the Creation: The Men Behind Postwar Germany's Defense and Intelligence Establishments* (Annapolis, Md.: Naval Institute Press, 2003), 86; Chief, OSO to Chief of Station, Karlsruhe, "Report of Investigation—RUSTY," December 17, 1948, Records of the Central Intelligence Agency, Record Group 263, RC box no. 2, 2000/06/02. Rusty was the American code name for the Gehlen Organization.

61. Erich Schmidt-Eenboom, "The Bundesnachrichtendienst, the Bundeswehr and Sigint in the Cold War and After," in *Secrets of Signals Intelligence During the Cold War and Beyond*, ed. Aid and Wiebes, 132, 136; Richard Helms, with

William Hood, *A Look over My Shoulder: A Life in the Central Intelligence Agency* (New York: Random House, 2003), 87. Helms was a senior CIA official responsible for Central Europe during this period.

62. Memorandum from Karlsruhe to Special Operations, Central Intelligence Group, December 17, 1948; Mary Ellen Reese, *General Reinhard Gehlen: The CIA Connection* (Fairfax, Va.: George Mason University Press, 1990), 50; Christopher Simpson, *Blowback: America's Recruitment of Nazis and Its Effects on the Cold War* (New York: Weidenfeld & Nicolson, 1988), 43, 63.

63. Critchfield, *Partners at the Creation*, 84.

64. Reese, *General Reinhard Gehlen*, 90–97; Critchfield, *Partners at the Creation*, 197.

65. "The Acting United States Political Advisor for Germany (Riddleberger) to the Secretary of State," February 12, 1948, in *FRUS 1948*, 2:875–76, Records of the Central Intelligence Agency, Record Group 263, RC box no. 2, 2000/06/02.

66. Quoted in T. H. Tetens, *Germany Plots with the Kremlin* (New York: Schuman, 1953), 105.

67. Central Intelligence Agency, "Political and Economic Changes in Western Europe Since the Last Conference of Foreign Ministers," ORE 58–49, June 1, 1949, in *CIA Research Reports*, reel 1, p. 15.

68. Central Intelligence Agency, "Germany," SR 20, December 9, 1949, in *CIA Research Reports*, reel 2, pp. iv–1.

69. Central Intelligence Agency, "Political Orientation of the West German State," ORE 1–50, April 25, 1950, in *CIA Research Reports*, reel 2, p. 1.

70. Konrad Adenauer, *Memoirs*, trans. Beate Ruhm von Oppen (Chicago: Regnery, 1966), 114. See also Eisenberg, *Drawing the Line*, 42–423.

71. Eisenberg, *Drawing the Line*.

72. "Teleconference," in *The Papers of General Lucius D. Clay: Germany, 1945–1949*, ed. Jean Edward Smith (Bloomington: Indiana University Press, 1974), 1102.

73. Thomas Alan Schwartz, *America's Germany: John J. McCloy and the Federal Republic of Germany* (Cambridge, Mass.: Harvard University Press, 1991), 56.

74. Headquarters, European Command, Intelligence Division, to Commanding Officer, 7821 Composite Group, "Operational Directive for the 7821 Composite Group," October 13, 1948; and Memorandum from Karlsruhe to Special Operations, Central Intelligence Group, December 17, 1948, both in Records of the Central Intelligence Agency, Record Group 263, RC box no. 2, 2000/06/02.

75. Helms, *Look over My Shoulder*, 89.

76. Critchfield, *Partners at the Creation*, 87.

77. Ibid., 127.

78. Reese, *General Reinhard Gehlen*, 107–11.

79. Helms, *Look over My Shoulder*, 89.

80. To Chief, FBM, "Current Situation," April 18, 1949; and Chief of Station, Karlsruhe to Chief, FBM, "Rusty," August 19, 1948, both in Records of the Central Intelligence Agency, Record Group 263, RC box no. 2, 2000/06/02.

81. Critchfield, *Partners at the Creation*, 157.

82. Memorandum for the Director, Central Intelligence, "Recommendations in re Operation Rusty," December 21, 1948; and Memorandum to Chief, FBM, "Dr. Schneider's Reply to Recent Policy Guidance Letters," October 12, 1949, both in Records of the Central Intelligence Agency, Record Group 263, RC box no. 2, 2000/06/02. Schneider was Gehlen's cover name at the CIA.

83. Breitman et al., *U.S. Intelligence and the Nazis*, 377.

3. INTELLIGENCE SHARING FOR COUNTERINSURGENCY

1. See, for example, Richard Clutterbuck, *The Long Long War: Counterinsurgency in Malaya and Vietnam* (New York: Praeger, 1966); Alistair Horne, *A Savage War of Peace* (New York: Viking, 1977); Frank Kitson, *Low Intensity Operations: Subversion, Insurgency and Peacekeeping* (London: Faber & Faber, 1971); John A. Nagl, *Learning to Eat Soup with a Knife: Counterinsurgency Lessons from Malaya to Vietnam* (Chicago: University of Chicago Press, 2005); Bard E. O'Neill, *Insurgency and Terrorism: Inside Modern Revolutionary Warfare* (Dulles, Va.: Brassey's, 1990); Kalev I. Sepp, "Best Practices in Counterinsurgency," *Military Review* 85 (2005): 8–12; Robert Taber, *War of the Flea: The Classic Study of Guerrilla Warfare* (Dulles, Va.: Potomac Books, 2002); and Robert Thompson, *Defeating Communist Insurgency: The Lessons of Malaya and Vietnam* (New York: Praeger, 1966), 85. The U.S. military's recent statement of counterinsurgency doctrine also emphasizes intelligence. See Department of the Army, *Counterinsurgency*, FM 3-24 (Washington, D.C.: Headquarters, Department of the Army, 2006).

2. See, especially, Clutterbuck, *Long Long War*, 99–106; and Thompson, *Defeating Communist Insurgency*, 99.

3. Andrew J. Krepinevich, *The Army in Vietnam* (Baltimore: Johns Hopkins University Press, 1986), 14–15; Nagl, *Learning to Eat Soup with a Knife*, xiv–xv; Jennifer Sims, "Foreign Intelligence Liaison: Devils, Deals, and Details," *International Journal of Intelligence and Counterintelligence* 19, no. 2 (2006): 195–217.

4. For example, the U.S. Army's recent counterinsurgency manual emphasizes the importance of the host nation's agencies for collecting intelligence but does not examine why such agencies might face incentives to avoid full sharing. See Department of the Army, *Counterinsurgency*, 61–62.

5. Douglas S. Blaufarb, *The Counterinsurgency Era: U.S. Doctrine and Performance, 1950 to the Present* (New York: Free Press, 1977); Daniel L. Byman, "Friends Like These: Counterinsurgency and the War on Terrorism," *International Security* 31, no. 2 (2006): 91–105; James T. Quinlivan, "Coup-proofing: Its Practice and Consequence in the Middle East," *International Security* 24, no. 2 (1999): 131–65.

6. Byman, "Friends Like These," 82.

7. Sam Adams, *War of Numbers: An Intelligence Memoir* (South Royalton, Vt.: Steerforth Press, 1994), 34, 54–61, 179–81; Dale Andradé, *Ashes to Ashes: The Phoenix Program and the Vietnam War* (Lexington, Mass.: Lexington Books, 1990), 222–25; Hoang Ngoc Lung, *The General Offensives of 1968–69* (Washington, D.C.: U.S. Army Center of Military History, 1978), 33–37; Mark Moyar, *Phoenix and the Birds of Prey: The CIA's Secret Campaign to Destroy the Viet Cong* (Annapolis, Md.: Naval Institute Press, 1997), 64–66.

8. George W. Allen, *None So Blind: A Personal Account of the Intelligence Failure in Vietnam* (Chicago: Ivan R. Dee, 2001), 219–26; James L. Gilbert, *The Most Secret War: Army Signals Intelligence in Vietnam* (Fort Belvoir, Va.: Military History Office, U.S. Army Intelligence and Security Command, 2003); Moyar, *Phoenix and the Birds of Prey*, 70; Gilles Van Nederveen, *Wizardry for Air Campaigns: Signals Intelligence Support to the Cockpit* (Maxwell Air Force Base, Montgomery, Ala.: Air University Press, 2001); Lewis Sorley, *A Better War: The Unexamined Victories and Final Tragedy of America's Last Years in Vietnam* (New York: Harcourt Brace, 1999), 47–53.

9. Allen, *None So Blind*, 178; George McT. Kahin, *Intervention: How America Became Involved in Vietnam* (New York: Anchor Books, 1987), 195–98; Lung, *General Offensives of 1968–69*, 1. Internal discussions of these issues by senior American officials include the views of Ambassador Maxwell Taylor, summarized in his "Memorandum of Meeting on Southeast Asia," November 27, 1964, in *Pentagon Papers: The Gravel Edition* (Boston: Beacon Press, 1971), 3:675; and John McNaughton, "Plan of Action for South Vietnam," September 3, 1964, in *Pentagon Papers*, 3:556–57. For an intelligence assessment, see NSC Working Group on Vietnam, "Section 1: Intelligence Assessment: The Situation in Vietnam," November 24, 1964, in *Pentagon Papers*, 3:651–56.

10. Guenter Lewy, *America in Vietnam* (New York: Oxford University Press, 1978), 92, 185; Richard A. Hunt, *Pacification: The American Struggle for Vietnam's Hearts and Minds* (Boulder, Colo.: Westview Press, 1995), 37.

11. Neil Sheehan, "CIA Says Enemy Spies Hold Vital Posts in Saigon," *New York Times*, October 19, 1970.

12. Larry E. Cable, *Conflict of Myths: The Development of American Counterinsurgency Doctrine and the Vietnam War* (New Haven, Conn.: Yale University Press, 1986), 249; Kahin, *Intervention*, 207; Lewy, *America in Vietnam*, 19, 87,

163; "US–GVN Relations, 1964–1967," in *Pentagon Papers*, 2:311–14; "American Troops Enter the Ground War, March–July 1965," in *Pentagon Papers*, 3:428; Sorley, *Better War*, 186–87; Shelby L. Stanton, *The Rise and Fall of an American Army: U.S. Ground Forces in Vietnam, 1965–1973* (Novato, Calif.: Presidio Press, 1985), 82–83; James J. Wirtz, *The Tet Offensive: Intelligence Failure in War* (Ithaca, N.Y.: Cornell University Press, 1991), 116. See also Secretary of Defense, "Memorandum for the President, Subject: South Vietnam," March 16, 1964, in *Pentagon Papers*, 3:499–509.

13. Quoted in Lung, *General Offensives of 1968–69*, 41. Other information in this paragraph is from Allen, *None So Blind*, 171; Andradé, *Ashes to Ashes*, 50, 62; Hunt, *Pacification*, 113; and Moyar, *Phoenix and the Birds of Prey*, 83, 130; an internal statement on these issues is Central Intelligence Agency, "The Intelligence Attack on the Viet Cong Infrastructure," May 23, 1967, Komer–Leonhart File, box 11, ICEX, National Security File, Papers of Lyndon B. Johnson, Lyndon B. Johnson Library, Austin, Tex.

14. Kahin, *Intervention*, 188, 199, 405.

15. Andradé, *Ashes to Ashes*, 83. See also William Colby, *Lost Victory* (Chicago: Contemporary Books, 1989), 256.

16. Douglas S. Blaufarb, *The Counterinsurgency Era: U.S. Doctrines and Performance* (New York: Free Press, 1977); Cable, *Conflict of Myths*; Hunt, *Pacification*; Kahin, *Intervention*, 347–65; Robert W. Komer, *Bureaucracy at War: U.S. Performance in the Vietnam Conflict* (Boulder, Colo.: Westview Press, 1986); Krepinevich, *Army in Vietnam*; and Nagl, *Learning to Eat Soup with a Knife*.

17. Lewy, *America in Vietnam*, 122. See also Andradé, *Ashes to Ashes*, 62–63; Wirtz, *Tet Offensive*, 18; and Krepinevich, *Army in Vietnam*, 194–95. McNamara accepted Westmoreland's argument. See Secretary of Defense, "Memorandum for the President, Subject: South Vietnam," March 16, 1964, 509.

18. Bruce E. Jones, *War Without Windows* (New York: Vanguard Press, 1987), 65–66; Moyar, *Phoenix and the Birds of Prey*, 67–88; Wirtz, *Tet Offensive*, 92–93, 97. See also Joseph A. McChristian, *The Role of Military Intelligence, 1965–1967* (Washington, D.C.: Department of the Army, 1994); and Ngo Quang Truong, *RVNAF and United States Operational Cooperation and Coordination* (Washington, D.C.: U.S. Army Center of Military History, 1979). McChristian was the assistant chief of staff for intelligence, U.S. Military Assistance Command, South Vietnam; and Truong was a senior South Vietnamese military officer during this period.

19. Discussions of the shift in American policy from search and destroy to pacification include Andradé, *Ashes to Ashes*; Blaufarb, *Counterinsurgency Era*; Hunt, *Pacification*; Edward P. Metzner, "More Than a Soldier's War: Pacification in Vietnam," in *Pentagon Papers*, 3:55; and Neil Sheehan, *A Bright Shining Lie: John Paul Vann and America in Vietnam* (New York: Vintage Books, 1989).

Pacification was a policy objective before 1967, but after this, it received much more high-level attention, increased resources, and more aggressive pressure on the South Vietnamese government to ensure that it was implemented.

20. See, for example, Robert Komer to William Westmoreland, "Organization for Attack on V.C. Infrastructure," 1, Komer–Leonhart File, box 11, ICEX, National Security File, Papers of Lyndon B. Johnson, Lyndon B. Johnson Library (italics added). Other, similar reports are summarized in Komer, *Bureaucracy at War*, 33.

21. The number of advisers jumped from about 1,000 in 1966 to more than 7,600 in 1969. Roughly 85 percent were military advisers, and the remainder worked for civilian branches of the U.S. government. See Jeffrey J. Clarke, *Advice and Support: The Final Years, 1965–1973* (Washington, D.C.: Center for Military History, 1988), 373.

22. Andradé, *Ashes to Ashes*, 86–90; Hunt, *Pacification*, 116–20. For a discussion of how South Vietnamese commanders pressed advisers to forward only positive reports, see Colby, *Lost Victory*, 257.

23. Central Intelligence Agency, "The President's Trip to Guam, March 1967: RD/Pacification Program (Cadre)," March 18, 1967, Paul Warnke Papers, box 5, Lyndon B. Johnson Library; Allen, *None So Blind*, 21–226; Andradé, *Ashes to Ashes*, 165–66; Colby, *Lost Victory*, 268, 279; Hunt, *Pacification*, 14–15; Komer, *Bureaucracy at War*, 33, 37, 120; Moyar, *Phoenix and the Birds of Prey*, 82.

24. Komer to Westmoreland, "Organization for Attack on V.C. Infrastructure"; Andradé, *Ashes to Ashes*, 65–68, 209; Moyar, *Phoenix and the Birds of Prey*, 98–99, Lewy, *America in Vietnam*, 280.

25. "Special National Intelligence Estimate SNIE 14–69," January 16, 1969, and "Summary of Interagency Responses to NSSM 1," March 22, 1969, both in Department of State, *FRUS 1969–1976*, vol. 6, *Vietnam, January 1969–July 1970* (Washington, D.C.: Government Printing Office, 2006); Military Assistance Command, *Vietnam, Phoenix: 1969 End of Year Report*, February 28, 1970, and *Vietnam, 1971 Command History*, vol. 1 (Saigon: USMACV Military History Branch, April 25, 1972).

26. A detailed and balanced assessment is Dale Andradé and James H. Willbanks, "CORDS/Phoenix: Counterinsurgency Lessons from Vietnam for the Future," *Military Review*, March–April 2006, 77–91.

27. Scott Sigmund Gartner, "Differing Evaluations of Vietnamization," *Journal of Interdisciplinary History* 29, no. 2 (1998): 243–62.

28. Detailed analyses of this experience include Brooks R. Brewington, "Combined Action Platoons: A Strategy for Peace Enforcement," Small Wars Center of Excellence, U.S. Marine Corps, 1996; Michael E. Hennessy, *Strategy in Vietnam: The Marines and Revolutionary Warfare in I Corps, 1965–1972* (Westport, Conn.: Praeger, 1997); Krepinevitch, *Army in Vietnam*; and Michael E. Peterson,

The Combined Action Platoons: The U.S. Marines' Other War in Vietnam (Westport, Conn.: Praeger, 1989).

29. William W. Go, "The Marine Corps' Combined Action Program and Modern Peace Operations," Small Wars Center of Excellence, U.S. Marine Corps, 1997.

30. For the experience in one village, see Francis J. West, *The Village* (Madison: University of Wisconsin Press, 1972); for a contrary experience, see Edward Palm, "Tiger Papa Three: A Memoir of the Combined Action Program, Part 1," *Marine Corps Gazette*, January 1988.

31. Good overviews of the conflict include Daniel W. Christman and John G. Heimann, *Andes 2020: A New Strategy for the Challenges of Colombia and the Region* (New York: Council on Foreign Relations, 2004); Russell Crandall, *Driven by Drugs: U.S. Policy Toward Colombia* (Boulder, Colo.: Lynne Rienner, 2002); Alexandra Guaqueta, "Change and Continuity in U.S.–Colombian Relations and the War Against Drugs," *Journal of Drug Issues* 11 (2005): 27–56; Victor J. Hinojosa, *Domestic Politics and International Narcotics Control: U.S. Relations with Mexico and Colombia, 1989–2000* (New York: Routledge, 2007); Mario A. Murillo, *Colombia and the United States: War, Unrest and Destabilization* (New York: Seven Stories Press, 2004); and Angel Rabasa and Peter Chalk, *Colombian Labyrinth: The Synergy of Drugs and Insurgency and Its Implications for Regional Stability* (Santa Monica, Calif.: RAND, 2001).

32. Gonzalo de Francisco Z, "Armed Conflict and Public Security in Colombia," in *Public Security and Police Reform in the Americas*, ed. John Bailey and Lucia Dammert (Pittsburgh: University of Pittsburgh Press, 2006), 96; Maria Victoria Llorente, "Demilitarization in a War Zone," in *Public Security and Police Reform in the Americas*, ed. Bailey and Dammert, 126; Peter Waldmann, "Colombia and the FARC: Failed Attempts to Stop Violence and Terrorism in a Weak State," in *Democracy and Terrorism*, ed. Robert Art and Louise Richardson (Washington, D.C.: United States Institute of Peace, 2006), 227–32.

33. Connie Veillette, "Plan Colombia: A Progress Report," *CRS Report for Congress*, February 17, 2005.

34. Guaqueta, "Change and Continuity in U.S.–Colombian Relations."

35. Andrés F. Sáenz and Ismael Idrobo, "Asking the Right Questions: The Evolution of Strategic Intelligence Discourse in Colombia," in *Intelligence Professionalism in the Americas*, ed. Russell G. Swenson and Susana C. Lemozy (Washington, D.C.: National Defense Intelligence College, 2003), 517.

36. Mark Bowden, *Killing Pablo* (New York: Atlantic Monthly Press, 2001).

37. Crandall, *Driven by Drugs*, 147; Waldmann, "Colombia and the FARC," 241–50.

38. See, for example, Amnesty International, *Amnesty International Annual Report* (London: Amnesty International Publications, 2003); and Department of

State, *2000 Country Reports on Human Rights Practices: Colombia* (Washington, D.C.: Department of State, 2001).

39. State Department cable, "Requests for Further EUM [End-Use Monitoring] Information Regarding COLAR [Colombian Army] 12th Brigade," March 27, 1998, confidential; and State Department cable, "Approach to MOD [Minister of Defense] on 24th Brigade," July 5, 2000, secret, both available at http://www.gwu.edu/%7Ensarchiv/NSAEBB/NSAEBB69/part3.html.

40. Central Intelligence Agency, "Colombia: Paramilitaries Assuming a Higher Profile," August 31, 1998, secret, available at http://www.gwu.edu/%7Ens archiv/NSAEBB/NSAEBB69/part3.html.

41. Crandall, *Driven by Drugs*, 117–18, 101–6; Waldmann, "Colombia and the FARC," 225, 235.

42. Crandall, *Driven by Drugs*, 106–7, 117–18.

43. Pamela Hess, "DOD to Shift Counter-Terror to Colombia," United Press International, September 24, 2002; Scott Wilson, "Hunt Expands for Missing Americans in Colombia," *Washington Post*, February 16, 2003; Jim Mannion, "U.S. to Resume Drug Flight Interdictions with Colombia," Agence France-Press, August 20, 2003.

44. Rowan Scarborough, "U.S. Helps Colombia Take Down Guerrillas," *Washington Times*, December 8, 2003; Andrew Skelsky, "U.S. Special Forces to Train Colombian Army Commandos," Associated Press, October 3, 2002.

45. Sáenz and Idrobo, "Asking the Right Questions."

46. Juan Forero, "New Role for U.S. in Colombia: Protecting a Vital Oil Pipeline," *New York Times*, October 4, 2002; Skelsky, "U.S. Special Forces."

47. Hess, "DOD to Shift Counter-Terror"; General Richard B. Myers, press conference, Bogotá, Colombia, August 12, 2003.

4. Intelligence Sharing in the European Union

1. Alain Guyomarch, "Cooperation in the Fields of Policing and Judicial Affairs," in *New Challenges to the European Union*, ed. Stelios Stavridis (Aldershot: Dartmouth); Bill Hebenton and Terry Thomas, *Policing Europe: Cooperation, Conflict, and Control* (London: St. Martin's Press, 1995); J. Peek, "International Police Cooperation Within Justified Political and Judicial Frameworks: Five Theses on Trevi," in *The Third Pillar of the European Union: Cooperation in the Fields of Justice and Home Affairs*, ed. Jorg Monar and Roger Morgan (Brussels: Interuniversity Press, 1994), 201–8; François Thuillier, *L'Europe du secret: Mythes et réalité du renseignement politique interne* (Paris: Institut des hautes études de la sécurité intérieure, 2000).

2. John Occhipinti, *The Politics of EU Police Cooperation: Toward a European FBI?* (Boulder, Colo.: Lynne Rienner, 2003), 121.

3. Thérèse Delpech, *Le Terrorisme international et l'Europe*, Cahiers de Chaillot 56 (Paris: European Union Institute for Security Studies, 2002).

4. Council of the European Union, "Brussels European Council Presidency Conclusions," June 18, 2004, 4; Secretary General, High Representative for the Common Foreign and Security Policy of the European Union, "Summary of Remarks by Javier Solana," SO159/04, June 8, 2004.

5. Occhipinti, *Politics of EU Police Cooperation*, 32; Rachel Woodward, "Establishing Europol," *European Journal on Criminal Policy and Research* 1, no. 4 (1994): 7–33.

6. A complete list can be found in Occhipinti, *Politics of EU Police Cooperation*, 192.

7. Quotations from Europol Convention, articles 3.1–3.2.

8. Björn Müller-Wille, "Building a European Intelligence Community in Response to Terrorism," *ISIS European Security Review*, April 2004.

9. Europol Convention, article 8. See also James B. Jacobs and Dimitra Blitsa, "Major 'Minor' Progress Under the Third Pillar: EU Institution Building in the Sharing of Criminal Record Information," *Chicago Kent Journal of International and Comparative Law* 8 (2008): 111–65.

10. Secretary General, High Representative for the Common Foreign and Security Policy, "Summary of Remarks by Javier Solana," SO159/04, June 8, 2004; Assembly of the West European Union, *The New Challenges Facing European Intelligence* (Paris: Assembly of the West European Union, June 4, 2002), par. 64–65; Giles Tremlett and Ian Black, "EU Plan to Pool Anti-Terrorism Intelligence," *Guardian*, March 2, 2002.

11. Gijs de Vries, "Discours pronounce devant la Commission des affairs étrangères de l'Assemblée nationale," June 22, 2004, 11 (my translation). See also Jean-Pierre Stroobants, "Les Vingt-cinq peaufinent leur stratégie antiterroriste," *Le Monde*, July 10, 2006.

12. Richard J. Aldrich, "Transatlantic Intelligence and Security Cooperation," *International Affairs* 80, no. 4 (2004): 739.

13. Europol Convention, article 10.7; these rules are elaborated in Council Act of 3 November 1998, Adopting Rules Applicable to Europol Analysis Files (1999/C 26/01).

14. Europol Convention, article 4.5.

15. Assembly of the West European Union, *New Challenges Facing European Intelligence*, par. 68, 72.

16. Björn Müller-Wille, "EU Intelligence Cooperation: A Critical Analysis," *Contemporary Security Policy* 23, no. 2 (2002): 76.

17. Frédéric Oberson, "Intelligence Cooperation in Europe: The WEU Intelligence Section and Situation Centre," in *Towards a European Intelligence Policy*,

ed. Alessandro Politi (Paris: Western European Union Institute for Security Studies, 1998).

18. Ole R. Villadsen, "Prospects for a European Common Intelligence Policy," *Studies in Intelligence* 44, no. 9 (2000): 81–94.

19. Assembly of the West European Union, *New Challenges Facing European Intelligence*, par. 89.

20. Swedish Security Service, *Annual Report* (Stockholm: Swedish Security Service, 2001), 31.

21. Council of the European Union, "Conclusions and Plan of Action of the Extraordinary European Council Meeting," September 21, 2001.

22. Ian Black, "On the Brink of War," *Guardian*, September 21, 2001.

23. "European Police Chief Says Only Scant Information Being Received from USA," BBC Monitoring Europe, September 15, 2001; Lisbeth Kirk, "Total Control Requires Total Surveillance," *EU Observer*, September 17, 2001.

24. Convention Européenne, Groupe du travail X. 2002, "Note de synthèse de la réunion du 25 septembre 2002," CONV 313/02, October 10, 2002.

25. "Ministers Revamp Anti-Terrorist Policies," *European Report*, March 20, 2004.

26. "EU Intelligence Sharing Must Be Mandatory," BBC Monitoring Service, March 19, 2004.

27. Ambrose Evans-Pritchard, "Time to Cut Waffle and Tackle Terror, Blunkett Tells EU," *Daily Telegraph*, March 20, 2004.

28. Other works that analyze hierarchy in the European Union include Katja Weber and Mark Hallerberg, "Explaining Variation in Institutional Integration in the European Union: Why Firms May Prefer European Solutions," *Journal of European Public Policy* 8, no. 2 (2001): 171–91; and Walter Mattli, *The Logic of Regional Integration: Europe and Beyond* (Cambridge: Cambridge University Press, 1999).

29. Charles Grant, *Intimate Relations* (London: Centre for European Reform, 2000).

30. The "intergovernmental" approach to the study of regional integration emphasizes that member states must be careful to agree to transfer authority to the European level only when it provides substantial benefits. Key works in this tradition are Stanley Hoffmann, "Obstinate or Obsolete: The Fate of the Nation State and the Case of Western Europe," *Daedalus* 95, no. 2 (1966): 862–915; and Andrew Moravcsik, "Preferences and Power in the EC: A Liberal Intergovernmentalist Approach," *Journal of Common Market Studies* 31, no. 4 (1993): 473–524, and *The Choice for Europe: Social Purpose and State Power from Messina to Maastricht* (Ithaca, N.Y.: Cornell University Press, 1998). Other approaches devote attention to other motives for transferring authority but acknowledge

that the member states' self-interested support remains crucial. See, for example, Paul Pierson, "The Path to European Integration: A Historical Institutionalist Account," *Comparative Political Studies* 29, no. 2 (1996): 123–63.

31. Among many, see Thomas Oatley, *Monetary Politics* (Ann Arbor: University of Michigan Press, 1997); or James I. Walsh, *European Monetary Integration and Domestic Politics* (Boulder, Colo.: Lynne Rienner, 2000).

32. Mattli, *Logic of Regional Integration*.

33. Good discussions include Lee Miles, "Moving Towards a Hub and Spokes Europe?" *Journal of Common Market Studies* 41, no. 1 (2003): 1–11; Alexander C.-G. Stubbs, "A Categorization of Differentiated Integration," *Journal of Common Market Studies* 34, no. 2 (2008): 283–95; and Neil Walker, "Sovereignty and Differentiated Integration in the European Union," *European Law Review* 4, no. 4 (2002): 355–88.

34. Thomas Ferenczi, "Terrorisme: Les cinq grads de l'UE veulent harmoniser les procedures d'expulsion," *Le Monde*, October 19, 2004.

35. George W. Downs, David M. Rocke, and Peter N. Barsoom, "Managing the Evolution of Multilateralism," *International Organization* 52, no. 2 (1998): 397–419.

36. "La France abrite une cellule antiterroriste secrète en plein Paris," *Le Monde*, September 13, 2006; "La Collaboration antiterroriste confirmée," Radio France, September 8, 2006, available at http://www.radiofrance.fr/reportage/laune/?rid=300000187#anc1.

5. Intelligence Sharing and U.S. Counterterrorism Policy

1. Derek S. Reveron, "Old Allies, New Friends: Intelligence-Sharing in the War on Terror," *Orbis* 50, no. 3 (2006): 455.

2. Daniel L. Byman, "Al-Qaeda as an Adversary: Do We Understand Our Enemy?" *World Politics* 56, no. 1 (2003): 154. See also Desmond Bell, "Desperately Seeking bin Ladin," in *Worlds in Collision: Terror and the Future of Global Order*, ed. Ken Booth and Tim Dunne (New York: Palgrave Macmillan, 2002).

3. Jeremy Pressman, "Rethinking Transnational Counterterrorism: Beyond a National Framework," *Washington Quarterly* 30, no. 4 (2007): 63–73.

4. Stéphane Lefebvre, "The Difficulties and Dilemmas of International Intelligence Cooperation," *International Journal of Intelligence and Counterintelligence* 16, no. 3 (2003): 527–42; Reveron, "Old Allies, New Friends"; Martin Rudner, "Hunters and Gatherers: The Intelligence Coalition Against Islamic Terrorism," *International Journal of Intelligence and Counterintelligence* 17, no. 1 (2004): 193–230.

5. Good discussions of other countries' willingness and ability to combat al Qaeda are Nora Bensahel, "A Coalition of Coalitions: International Cooperation Against Terrorism," *Studies in Conflict and Terrorism* 29, no. 1 (2006): 35–49; and Daniel Byman, "Remaking Alliances for the War on Terrorism," *Journal of Strategic Studies* 29, no. 5 (2006): 767–811.

6. Works that emphasize the importance of trust for effective intelligence sharing include Lefevre, "Difficulties and Dilemmas of International Intelligence Cooperation"; Richard Aldrich, "Transatlantic Intelligence and Security Cooperation," *International Affairs* 80, no. 4 (2004): 731–53; Chris Clough, "Quid Pro Quo: The Challenges of International Strategic Intelligence Cooperation," *International Journal of Intelligence and Counterintelligence* 17, no. 4 (2004): 601–13; and Bensahel, "Coalition of Coalitions."

7. The United States' national security strategy and the European Union's security strategy differ on many other issues but are remarkably similar in the importance they attach to counterterrorism. Compare "The National Security Strategy of the United States," September 2002, available at http://www .whitehouse.gov/nsc/nss.pdf, with "European Security Strategy," December 2003, available at http://www.consilium.europa.eu/uedocs/cmsUpload/78367.pdf.

8. Glen M. Segell, "Intelligence Agency Relations Between the European Union and the U.S.," *International Journal of Intelligence and Counterintelligence* 17, no. 1 (2004): 81–96.

9. Richard A. Clarke, Barry R. McCaffrey, and Richard C. Nelson, *NATO's Role in Confronting International Terrorism* (Washington, D.C.: Atlantic Council of the United States, 2004).

10. Lefevre, "Difficulties and Dilemmas of International Intelligence Cooperation"; Jennifer Sims, "Foreign Intelligence Liaison: Devils, Deals, and Details," *International Journal of Intelligence and Counterintelligence* 19, no. 2 (2006): 195–217.

11. Eric Schmitt, "New U.S. Law Credited in Arrests Abroad," *New York Times*, September 11, 2007; Michael C. Moss and Souad Mekhennet, "Glimpses of a Shadowy World in Pakistan," *New York Times*, September 17, 2007.

12. Elaine Sciolino, "From Tapes, a Chilling Voice of Islamic Radicalism in Europe," *New York Times*, November 18, 2005.

13. Dana Priest, "Help from France Key on Covert Operations: Paris's 'Alliance Base' Targets Terrorists," *Washington Post*, July 3, 2005.

14. Alan Cowell and Dexter Filkins, "Terror Plot Foiled; Airports Quickly Clamp Down," *New York Times*, August 11, 2006.

15. Elaine Sciolino and Don Van Atta, "With No Leads, British Consult Allies on Blasts," *New York Times*, July 11, 2005.

16. Priest, "Help from France"; "La France abrite une cellule antiterroriste secrète en plein Paris," *Le Monde*, September 13, 2006; "La Collaboration

antiterroriste confirmée," Radio France, September 8, 2006, available at http://www .radiofrance.fr/reportage/laune/?rid=300000187#anc1.

17. Council of Europe Parliamentary Committee on Legal Affairs and Human Rights, *Secret Detentions and Illegal Transfers of Detainees Involving Council of Europe Member States: Second Report* (Strasbourg: Council of Europe, June 7, 2007).

18. Stephen Gidler, "European Role in Secret US Flights Criticised," *Financial Times*, June 24, 2008.

19. Priest, "Help from France."

20. "EU Court Annuls Data Deal with US," BBC News, May 30, 2006, available at http://news.bbc.co.uk/2/hi/europe/5028918.stm; European Commission, "Airline Passenger Data Transfers from the EU to the United States," Memo/03/53, March 12, 2003, available at http://ec.europa.eu/external_relations/ us/intro/pnrmem03_53.htm.

21. Eric Lichtbau and James Risen, "Bank Data Is Sifted by U.S. in Secret to Block Terror," *New York Times*, June 23, 2007; Paul Blustein, Barton Gellman, and Dafna Linzer, "Bank Records Secretly Tapped," *Washington Post*, June 23, 2006; Constant Brand, "Belgian PM: Data Transfer Broke Rules," *Washington Post*, September 28, 2006; European Commission, "The SWIFT Case and the American Terrorist Finance Tracking Program," Memo/07/266, June 28, 2007, available at http://europa.eu/rapid/pressReleasesAction.do?reference=MEMO/07/266 &format=HTML&aged=1&language=EN&guiLanguage=en.

22. For example, the 2006 Corruption Perceptions Index, which compares perceptions of corruption in 163 countries, ranked Jordan as the fortieth least corrupt state, Egypt as the seventieth least corrupt state, and Morocco as the seventy-ninth least corrupt state. See Transparency International, "Corruption Perceptions Index 2006," available at http://www.transparency.org/policy_ research/surveys_indices/cpi/2006.

23. On government inaction toward Islamic terrorist groups, see Daniel Byman, *Deadly Connections: States That Sponsor Terrorism* (Cambridge: Cambridge University Press, 2005).

24. On the Egyptian origins of al Qaeda, see Gilles Kepel, *Jihad: The Trail of Political Islam* (Cambridge, Mass.: Belknap Press of Harvard University Press, 2003).

25. On support for terrorism, see Pew Global Attitudes Project, "The Great Divide: How Westerners and Muslims View Each Other," June 22, 2006, available at http://pewglobal.org/reports/display.php?ReportID=253. On attitudes toward the United States, see Pew Global Attitudes Project, "Global Unease with Major World Powers," June 27, 2007, available at http://pewglobal.org/reports/ display.php?ReportID=256.

26. Nathaniel Heller and Tom Stites, "Collateral Damage: The U.S. Hands Out Vast Sums of Money to Combat Terrorism While Ignoring Human Rights Records," Center for Public Integrity, May 22, 2007, available at http://www.publicintegrity.org/militaryaid/report.aspx?aid=872.

27. Ken Silverstein, "U.S. Partnership with Jordan Was Targeted," Los Angeles Times, November 12, 2005.

28. Craig Whitlock, "Jordan's Spy Agency: Holding Cell for the CIA," Washington Post, December 1, 2007; Amnesty International, "Jordan: Your Confessions Are Ready for You to Sign: Detention and Torture of Political Suspects," MDE 16/005/2006, July 24, 2006; Jane Mayer, "The Black Sites," New Yorker, August 2007; Joby Warrick and Dan Eggen, "Waterboarding Recounted," Washington Post, December 11, 2007; Silverstein, "U.S. Partnership with Jordan."

29. Dana Priest, "CIA Holds Terror Suspects in Secret Prisons," Washington Post, November 2, 2005.

30. Greg Miller, "Influx of Al Qaeda, Money into Pakistan Seen," Los Angeles Times, May 19, 2007; Moss and Mekhennet, "Glimpses of a Shadowy World in Pakistan."

31. Mark Mazzetti and Eric Schmitt, "C.I.A. Outlines Pakistan Links with Militants," New York Times, July 30, 2008; Joby Warrick, "U.S. Officials: Pakistani Agents Helped Plan Kabul Bombing," Washington Post, August 1, 2008.

32. David Rohde, "A Detour from a Battle Against Terror," New York Times, November 6, 2007.

33. Mark Mazzetti and David E. Sanger, "Bush Aides See Failure in Fight with al Qaeda in Pakistan," New York Times, July 17, 2007; Jane Perlez, "Militants Draw New Front Line Inside Pakistan," New York Times, November 1, 2007; Griff Witte, "Pakistan Seen Losing Fight Against Taliban and al Qaeda," Washington Post, October 3, 2007; U.S. Government Accounting Office, "Combating Terrorism: The United States Lacks Comprehensive Plan to Destroy the Terrorist Threat and Close the Safe Haven in Pakistan's Federally Administered Tribal Areas," GAO report GAO-08-622, 2008.

34. Craig Cohen and Derek Chollet, "When $10 Billion Is Not Enough: Rethinking U.S. Strategy Toward Pakistan," Washington Quarterly 30, no. 2 (2007): 7-19; David Rohde, Carlotta Gall, Eric Schmitt, and David E. Sanger, "U.S. Officials See Waste in Billions Sent to Pakistan," New York Times, December 24, 2007; Ann Scott Tyson, "U.S. to Step Up Training of Pakistanis," Washington Post, January 24, 2008.

35. David E. Sanger and David Rohde, "U.S. Pays Pakistan to Fight Terror, but Patrols Ebb," New York Times, May 20, 2007; Joby Warrick, "U.S. and Pakistan: A Frayed Alliance," Washington Post, October 31, 2007.

36. See, for example, Ismail Khan, "Missile Kills 5 in Northwest Pakistan; U.S. Denies Attack," *New York Times*, November 3, 2007; Eric Schmitt and David E. Sanger, "Pakistan Shift Could Curtail Drone Strikes," *New York Times*, February 22, 2008.

37. Steven Lee Myers, David E. Sanger, and Eric Schmitt, "U.S. Considers New Covert Push Within Pakistan," *New York Times*, January 6, 2008.

38. Lisa Martin, *Democratic Commitments: Legislatures and International Cooperation* (Princeton, N.J.: Princeton University Press, 2000); Xinyuan Dai, *International Institutions and National Policies* (Cambridge: Cambridge University Press, 2007).

39. Daniel L. Byman, "Friends Like These: Counterinsurgency and the War on Terrorism," *International Security* 31, no. 2 (2006): 82. See also Frank J. Cilluffo, Ronald A. Marks, and George C. Salmoiraghi, "The Use and Limits of U.S. Intelligence," *Washington Quarterly* 25, no. 1 (2002): 61–74.

40. Saxby Chambliss, "We Have Not Correctly Framed the Debate on Intelligence Reform," *Parameters*, spring 2005, 5–13.

41. *The 9/11 Commission Report: Final Report of the National Commission on Terrorist Attacks upon the United States* (Washington, D.C.: Government Printing Office, 2004), 415; Commission on the Intelligence Capabilities of the United States Regarding Weapons of Mass Destruction, *Report to the President of the United States* (Washington, D.C.: Government Printing Office, 2005).

6. FINDINGS AND IMPLICATIONS

1. Amy Zegart, "Cloaks, Daggers, and Ivory Towers: Why Academics Do Not Study U.S. Intelligence," in *Strategic Intelligence: Understanding the Hidden Side of Government*, vol. 1, ed. Loch K. Johnson (Westport, Conn.: Praeger, 2007).

2. See, for example, Uri-Bar Joseph and Rose McDermott, "Change the Analyst and Not the System: A Different Approach to Intelligence Reform," *Foreign Policy Analysis* 4, no. 2 (2008): 127–45; Thomas H. Hammond, "Why Is the Intelligence Community So Difficult to Redesign? Smart Practices, Conflicting Goals, and the Creation of Purpose-Built Organizations," *Governance* 20, no. 3 (2007): 401–22; and Amy Zegart, *Spying Blind: The CIA, the FBI, and the Origins of 9/11* (Princeton, N.J.: Princeton University Press, 2007).

3. On Iran, see Mark Gasiorowski, *U.S. Foreign Policy and the Shah: Building a Client State* (Ithaca, N.Y.: Cornell University Press, 1991); for Latin America, see J. Patrice McSherry, *Predatory States: Operation Condor and Covert War in Latin America* (Boulder, Colo.: Rowman & Littlefield, 2005); and for China, see Jeffrey Richelson and Desmond Ball, *The Ties That Bind* (New York: HarperCollins, 1986), and Harry Harding, *A Fragile Relationship: The United States and China*

Since 1972 (Washington, D.C.: Brookings Institution Press, 1992). Saudi Arabia is discussed in Derek Reveron, "Old Allies, New Friends: Intelligence Sharing in the War on Terror," *Orbis* 50, no. 3 (2006): 453–68. Central Asia is covered in Alexander Cooley, *Base Politics: Democratic Changes and the U.S. Military Overseas* (Ithaca, N.Y.: Cornell University Press, 2008).

4. C. William Walldorf Jr., "When Humanitarianism Matters: Liberalism and the Termination of Strategic Commitments," *Security Studies* 14, no. 2 (2005): 232–73.

5. See, in particular, *The 9/11 Commission Report: Final Report of the National Commission on Terrorist Attacks upon the United States* (Washington, D.C.: Government Printing Office, 2004); and Commission on the Intelligence Capabilities of the United States Regarding Weapons of Mass Destruction, *Report to the President of the United States* (Washington, D.C.: Government Printing Office, 2005). The latest plan for improving intelligence sharing is in Office of the Director of National Intelligence, *United States Intelligence Community Information Sharing Strategy* (Washington, D.C.: Office of the Director of National Intelligence, February 22, 2008).

6. Cogent discussions of organization reform are Richard K. Betts, *Enemies of Intelligence: Knowledge and Power in American National Security* (New York: Columbia University Press, 2007); and Zegart, *Spying Blind.*

7. Jason D. Ellis and Geoffrey D. Kiefer, *Combating Proliferation: Strategic Intelligence and Security Policy* (Baltimore: Johns Hopkins University Press, 2007); Commission on the Intelligence Capabilities of the United States Regarding Weapons of Mass Destruction, *Report to the President of the United States.*

8. Alexander H. Montgomery, "Ringing in Proliferation: How to Dismantle an Atomic Bomb Network," *International Security* 30, no. 2 (2005): 153–87.

9. Roberta Wohlstetter, *Pearl Harbor: Warning and Decision* (Stanford, Calif.: Stanford University Press, 1962).

10. Helen V. Milner argues that the same tools and ideas can often be used to analyze political interactions that are and are not characterized by formal anarchy, in "Rationalizing Politics: The Emerging Synthesis of International, American, and Comparative Politics," *International Organization* 52, no. 4 (1998): 759–86. Concepts from transaction costs economics have been applied extensively to questions in American politics, including relations among Congress, the presidency, and the bureaucracy. For an overview, see Gary J. Miller, "The Political Evolution of Principal-Agent Models," *Annual Review of Political Science* 8 (2005): 203–25.